Being Prayer

Transforming Consciousness

This work is a wealth of information for those on the journey toward higher consciousness. There is something pertinent for all regardless of spiritual leanings or methods of meditation. The readers will connect with it based on their own experience and practice, reflecting the principle that all things of a higher nature come when one is ready to receive them.

—MARY HENDRICKS, MS, RYT
Yoga Alliance of Registered Yoga Teachers

Being Prayer

Transforming Consciousness

Good News of Buddhist Practice

MARY REES

2006

NUTSHELL PUBLICATIONS™
HOUSTON, TX

NUTSHELL PUBLICATIONS
PO BOX 20161, HOUSTON, TX 77025

ISBN-13: 978-0-9760036-7-0
ISBN-10: 0-9760036-7-8

Library of Congress Control Number: 2006901542

 Printed on recycled paper in the United States.

Grateful acknowledgment is made of the following sources:

Quotation at beginning of chapter 2: From Thomas Merton's "Restricted Journals of 1956–1968" as quoted by Michael Mott, *The Seven Mountains of Thomas Merton*, 545. Copyright 1984.

Epigraph at beginning of chapter 3: From J. Krishnamurti, *The First and Last Freedom*, 135. Copyright 1954. Reprinted by permission of the Krishnamurti Foundation of America.

Poem at beginning of chapter 5: From Matthew Fox, ed., *Meditations with Meister Eckhart*, 10. Copyright 1982. Reprinted by permission of Dennis Edwards.

"The Kalamas's Dilemma" in the Epilogue: Adapted from *Anguttara Nikaya* and reprinted by permission of Andrew Olendzki, translator and adaptor, Barre Center for Buddhist Studies.

Good News

Teaching of Jesus Christ

Surrender:
The Kingdom is Now.

Teaching of Gautama Buddha

Surrender:
Nothing is as substantial as it appears to be.

The potentiality of the next moment is totally open,
conditioned by our interaction with this one.

CONTENTS

❧◯◯☙

Foreword

Both the Buddha and Jesus Christ offered the teachings that they did in order to help people change themselves for the better. In this small book Mary Rees brings together, in particular, a number of essential Buddhist-based practices which can help to effect such positive changes, yet which are cast in a language and form that also renders them highly useable by those of a Christian faith — indeed, of any religious faith at all.

I greatly respect Mary's endeavor — to elucidate some parallels that these two great spiritual traditions possess, to foster understanding between them, and, most importantly, to make their contemplative practices more accessible to the general public — and in this I'm reminded of an occasion when His Holiness the Dalai Lama was invited to give commentaries on the Christian Gospels. I was fortunate enough to be present at that John Main Seminar in London, in 1994, and heard His Holiness, in his inimitably self-effacing fashion, begin by saying that he knew very little about Christianity but that, since the organisers didn't seem to be at all put off by that fact, he was happy to share his thoughts on the passages they had suggested. Following this, and most significantly, he said that he saw it as his job to help the audience (comprised mostly of Christian meditators) be more confirmed in their Christian faith. He memorably stated that if, by offering his reflections from a Buddhist perspective, he caused any of those present to become less secure in their commitment to their religion, he would feel that he had failed in his task. Needless to say, the result of his expressing this was that everyone in the hall had more faith in his wisdom than ever before.

I was greatly impressed at that time by His Holiness' attitude and I would like to echo it here: even though this book contains mostly

Buddhist teachings, its intent should not be seen as that of conversion or an attempt to weaken the faith of practising Christians — rather, it is the opposite. Hopefully the insights and practices contained herein will serve to support the contemplative life and deepen the heart of faith, whatever that faith may be, in all those whose eyes imbibe the words on these pages.

The world that we live in, in 2005, is a place of great fertility and wonder, as well as being a place of great conflict, deprivation, and environmental destruction. The causes of much of this difficulty are the choices we make as individuals, day by day, hour by hour. What this humble book is offering is a collection of trainings in attitudes and practices that can directly affect our own hearts and help us to make wiser choices — thus reducing the causes of ignorance, conflict, sectarianism, and selfishness within us.

As human beings we learn and teach primarily by example; therefore, if we are still in a state of anxious confusion whilst we attempt to serve and straighten out the world, our energies are bound to become scattered, and people's confidence in us will wane. Therefore, from the Buddhist perspective at least, helping yourself first is a sine qua non in order to be of true service to others. This principle is displayed in an oft-quoted passage from the Buddhist scriptures:

> *"Monks, once in the past an acrobat set up his bamboo pole and addressed his apprentice Frying Pan thus: 'Come, dear Frying Pan, climb the bamboo pole and stand on my shoulders.' Having replied, 'Yes, teacher,' the apprentice Frying Pan climbed up the bamboo pole; then she stood on the teacher's shoulders. The acrobat then said to the apprentice Frying Pan: 'You protect me, dear Frying Pan, and I'll protect you. Thus guarded by one another, protected by one another, we'll display our skills, collect our fee, and get down safely from the bamboo pole.' When this was said, the apprentice Frying Pan replied: 'That's not the way to do it, teacher. You protect yourself, teacher, and I'll protect myself. Thus, each self-guarded and self-protected, we'll display our skills, collect our fee, and get down safely from the bamboo pole.'*

"That's the method there," the Buddha said. "It's just as the apprentice Frying Pan said to her teacher. 'I will protect myself,' monks: thus should the foundations of mindfulness be practised. 'I will protect others,' monks: thus should the foundations of mindfulness be practised. Protecting oneself, monks, one protects others; protecting others, one protects oneself.

"And how is it, monks, that by protecting oneself one protects others? By the pursuit, development, and cultivation of the four foundations of mindfulness. It is in such a way that by protecting oneself one protects others.

"And how is it, monks, that by protecting others one protects oneself? By patience, harmlessness, loving-kindness, and sympathy. It is in such a way that by protecting others one protects oneself."

—Sedaka Sutta, A 4.95

This teaching came to mind in a particularly vivid way when, soon after receiving Mary's manuscript in August, she contacted me for some guidance, as she had just been asked to counsel evacuees from New Orleans, gathered in their huddled thousands in the Houston Astrodome. Unwittingly, some of the advice I gave her that day (e.g. keep your attention in your body) bore a close resemblance to some of her own teachings contained within this book.

Not all the situations where we are called upon to offer our assistance are quite so extreme — it's usually more along the lines of being asked to pay attention to one of our family members — nevertheless, the kind of principle displayed here is one that this book helps to elucidate: when we heartfully care for our own realm of mind and body, cultivating peace and wisdom there, this is the most beneficial gift we can offer to the world.

May this book serve well in helping these principles come to life.

—AJAHN AMARO
Abhayagiri, Oct 7th 2005

Preface

Life can become dance, a joyful exercise of balance. In the most challenging circumstances we learn to stay with our experience, neither running away nor fighting. We choose instead to be mindfully aware and to surrender to what is, accepting life just as it is. We live on the vital edge of things, avoiding the heresy of stepping down on the extreme of one side or the other of philosophical or theological truths. And, most importantly, we learn to do this, not conceptually, but experientially. We become truth, experiencing it in and through our bodies, manifesting truth and tender heart qualities in our daily lives.

Most of the practices offered here are those taught early in the tradition we now know as Buddhism. They are amenable to any spiritual practice in any tradition. They are devoid of the transformations and embellishments of many centuries of cultural evolution, an evolutionary process that creates traditions appropriate for different times and circumstances. This morphing potential is an integral element and one of the great beauties of these teachings.

The sophisticated philosophies and theologies that evolve are important and valuable, worthy of deep investigation. However, at the heart of the teachings are basic practices that are easily transplanted. It is through personal experience with, and dedication to, these basic practices that transformation occurs and from which the deepest wisdom can manifest uniquely in any cultural setting and in each human being.

Through these practices we help create space for enlightened moments to occur in which something totally unexpected, genuinely loving, and joyful happens, space in which behaviors arise that are much more powerful, wise, and skillful than we are capable of coming to by using linear mind alone. We open to a life of spontaneous compassion, in harmony with the planet and all living things.

The work presented here is my responsibility, a culmination of my life experience to this point, as well as another beginning. However, what has emerged is due to the dynamics of many relationships and to a fundamental goodness in the universe.

I can't name all the contributors to my understanding. The bibliography is a beginning, as is the list of teachers I have worked with that can be found on my website.

The perspective here is offered in gratitude for all who have contributed to its evolution: teachers and their teachers before them, especially Marcia Rose, Rodney Smith, Sisters Mary Dennison and Alice Meenan, and Father Ed Abell; students, without whom there would be no teacher; editors Roger Leslie and Mary Sieber and graphic designer Kristin Kearns; friends and family, especially Con and Nathan (husband and son).

May all of the fruits of this work be wholesome.

May its merits contribute to the peace and happiness, health, strength, and deep ease of being of all creatures everywhere, without exception.

— M. R.
May 21, 2005

Being Prayer

Transforming Consciousness

Introduction

This is the path of transcendence:
transcending the mortal condition,
through awareness of the mortal condition.

—AJAHN SUMEDHO

The most powerful prayer is not just something we do. It is something we are. All of life can be one continuous prayer, a connectedness with all beings and a deep union with Mystery, a surrender to a new way of being and living in the world. Being Prayer comes about through a transformation of consciousness in which we let the most profound theological and philosophical teachings, through simple bodily practices, manifest a deep and wholesome spirituality in any moment of life.

If we begin to think of all life and every action as prayer, then meditation skills and Buddhist practices offer not only ways to pray, but also ways we actually become prayer in our body and way of being.

If listening deeply and being radically open are fundamental to prayer, then meditation is precisely the tool for deepening receptivity.

If the possibility of a direct connection with Love and Wisdom can be understood to be prayer, then meditation teachings, especially those in the Buddhist traditions, offer a vast array of practices and paths for opening to these profound qualities.

If learning to be kinder, wiser, and more compassionate is prayer, then meditation is a powerful way to bring us to our greatest potential, to a manifestation of our personalities as both ordinary and extraordinary, and, from a Christian perspective, both human and divine.

As prayer we become the conscious meeting point and mediating space of multiple dimensions of existence. In fact, prayer from this perspective includes awareness of all existence as fullness and everything as interdependent, connected, and interwoven. We come to the realization of our oneness with this vastness and find ourselves to be, like all other beings, unique manifestations of it in each particular moment.

The human experience and human potential are highly valued in both Buddhist and Christian traditions. The Buddhists consider human life a very rare and precious opportunity, largely because it is in human form that one can most efficiently and effectively do spiritual practice. It is in human form, with human reflexive consciousness, that we can look at our own mind and intervene in its processes! As we do so, we attain freedom from ignorance, from craving, and therefore from suffering. We unfold into deeper spirituality and expanded states of consciousness. We evolve in greater wisdom and compassion. We become kinder and are less likely to cause harm to others or ourselves. We are happy, content, and at ease in life.

The central Christian message, in inspired understanding, is that humanity can actually manifest as divinity. Jesus was the first human being to do this. He led the way and made it possible for others to follow.[1] The crucifixion and resurrection of Jesus are primary symbols or manifestations of this possibility. Jesus' whole life was surrender, kindness, and simplicity. Though he is understood to have had human emotions and even to have expressed anger, he refused to respond to violence with violence or with other forms of harm. His crucifixion was an ultimate surrender that led to resurrection, to wholeness, and to new life.

Though the nuances in understanding this event divide Christians into different camps (within traditions rather than between them), from the perspective I'm sharing of surrender as a way to new life, we see Jesus as a very human person, one who has come to fullness in both the divine and human aspects of his being. In him divinity and humanity are no longer two separate ways of being. He lives from a wider, fuller perspective.

Jesus provides a powerfully gentle model. His death and resurrection dramatically demonstrate, through one physical body, the power of surrender. We can learn from this example, not to die physically, as was the understanding of early Christian martyrs, but to surrender through moment-to-moment dying to the sense of self. We can challenge the pride in clinging to our own perspective. As we do so, we can become whole and, from this Christian perspective, elevated to living as both human and divine.[2] We don't replace God, but join in co-creating a loving world. From a Buddhist perspective, we wake up.

Surrender and resurrection are the central Christian teachings for becoming Eucharist, for being sacrament.[3] We surrender and let ourselves become radically changed. We give up life-denying, unskillful, or unwholesome pursuits and instead hunger for and open to what is deeply satisfying — a living awareness of, and connection with, Mystery and all beings everywhere. We become aware that our fate and our behaviors are connected with those of the planet and of the universe. To use powerful Christian imagery: we choose to become bread for the world, broken and shared.

There is no room for violence in this understanding. Through vulnerability we are our strongest. In appropriate surrender, surrender with mindfulness, we not only bring the strength that naturally occurs through mindfulness, but also allow a greater power than our ordinary mind to manifest in the world through us. We die figuratively (before we die literally) and then live more fully.

The understanding of appropriate surrender is important. We do not denigrate ourselves. We do not intentionally seek suffering, certainly not death, nor do we accept living in relationships or communities that are harmful to us. On the contrary, we open to a great joy or contentment that is available to us in even the most difficult circumstances. We become attentive to our immediate experience and become free of grasping and aversion, of limiting views and opinions. Problems and life's difficulties do not disappear, but our relationship to them is dramatically altered. We participate responsibly, but we no longer suffer by trying to control or to stop inevitable change from occurring.

The Buddhist teachings offer practices of continual opening and transformation, not usually occurring once and forever, but in small experiences at a time, moment by moment. Through awareness, release, letting go, and through attention to experience, we come to self-knowledge, discovering that we are not what we thought ourselves to be. We are less substantial, but also less limited, much fuller and richer. We are innately capable of being spacious and expansive, wise and compassionate, joyful and happy.

We come to an experiential awareness of our interconnectedness, learning that we are part of a great web of life in which every action, event, or thought impacts the whole and in which any cultural progress is made only in connection with each other.

We work with our own experience, primarily through mindful attention and mindful awareness. We become more integrated and participate in life more skillfully. Opening the heart with attention and awareness, molding and shaping the mind, we consciously participate in our evolutionary process.

Buddhist practices aren't the only ways to pray or transform, but they are an excellent experiential foundation for coming to communion and to apprehension of our being, to prayer as all of life. Though there are devotional Buddhists who turn to enlightened beings for help and support, those beings are not usually seen as gods, as in the various Christian understandings of God. Buddhism is not theistic — at least it isn't intended to be. There is no savior to turn to even in times of great fear or desperation. The result is that Buddhists have spent lifetimes learning how to help themselves and have done so with great sophistication and subtlety.

Participating in our own transformation through the skills of a nontheistic tradition such as Buddhism need not exclude a savior. We can borrow these ancient and skillful means without offending anyone, adhering to any delineated dogma, or meeting prerequisite beliefs. We are welcome to explore, to come and see for ourselves. In fact, in Buddhist practice it is considered most unskillful to blindly accept teachings without exploring them in one's own experience.[4] The teachings are an invitation to a thorough experiential investigation into what is true, into what brings happiness, and what causes suffering. A great beauty of Buddhist practice is that it leaves the transcendent a mystery, thus making room for God without definition or limitation, without creating false images.

How do we become prayer?
How do we learn to be prayer?

A human being can be thought of as a continuum of experience or a moving matrix, a continuously flowing and changing point where transcendent and mundane meet. By learning to recognize and reside in this flowing and mediating space, we make openings through our very own body and being for nothing less than interpenetration of the transcendent into worldly affairs. We become prayer.

Perhaps this sounds difficult or magical. It is in some ways extraordinary, yet living in mediating space or being prayer is actually a practical and quite ordinary way to be.

Elucidating some methods for living this way is the primary purpose of this book, introducing experiential and investigative practices to help us learn to live as integrated beings. Most practices are directed toward finding what is true in any moment. In order to do this, the book offers an expanded understanding of what mind or consciousness is and of the powerful work involved in knowing consciousness and in freeing and molding the mind so as to allow the fullness of its unfolding.

Reading this text without experimenting with the practices will yield little result. A genuine grasp of the teachings requires both exploration of ideas and direct experience. In fact, information about the structure or the philosophical underpinnings has little use without the direct experience. Through exploring and investigating we can come to trust our own experience, letting direct contact with life be our primary teacher. It is especially in contact with our sensual selves that we can open to the vast truth beyond what is apparent, to that which is beneath or above language and the conceptual.[5]

Language, concepts, and abstract thinking are powerful, valuable, and essential tools; however, they can easily become traps, separating us from directly contacting life. The practices I share here are intended to bring us into direct contact with ordinary experience and with what I understand the fundamental purpose of all religious or spiritual practice to be — coming in contact with the true nature of reality, Ultimate Reality.

Spiritual practice as an exploratory process for realizing Ultimate Reality requires an intimate mindfulness, a deep investigation of experience, and an openness to transformational possibilities. Both Jesus and Gautama were well versed in their own cultural and spiritual traditions, but neither dogmatically accepted those teachings. Instead, they asked questions and explored. Both opened to a vital and dynamic process, joining their own lived experience with their understanding of transcendent truths. Each became a deeply human and fully realized being.

Discovering for ourselves this way of being is a precious and joyful way to live that opens to us a great journey of adventure and mystery. I offer here specific methods drawn primarily, but not exclusively, from Buddhist teachings; however, they are only a taste of the vast possibilities.

Each chapter ends with some recommended practices and reading. Among the appendices is an extensive, but not exhaustive reference list that includes recommended reading by related themes or threads. There is also an alphabetical bibliography at the end of the book. My intention is to make it easier to explore by providing a very loose structure that incorporates some of the breadth of Buddhist practice and includes a wide array of reliable resources from both spiritual and secular sources.

Work with these practices can bring wisdom and understanding, compassion, lightness of heart, and deep ease of being. Such spiritual maturity requires the courage to develop trust in one's own heart, for ultimately we must each determine the validity of teachings for ourselves and the direction to go with them. As you become familiar with the great range of possibilities, you will find and further explore teachings and practices according to your personal needs and process.

I hope that this book will be an inspiration for your deepening spiritual practice, a springboard for further exploration. The text will expand in meaning as you integrate the teachings into your own lived experiences. Consider returning periodically to the text to refresh your understanding and to see if some different part now stands out or has gained in significance. You might find in retrospect that prayer has become more of who you are.

CHAPTER ONE

Coming Home Through Our Senses

Just to be is a blessing,
Just to live is holy.

—ABRAHAM HESCHEL

I am sitting in the middle of a difficult experience — between two seemingly impossible circumstances, beyond any hope of resolving issues myself. Sometimes I'm burning in anger or puffed up and righteous, other times collapsed into inconsolable grief. Every cell in my body passes through the same range of experience, from rigid contractions to puddles of uselessness.

The environment mirrors my struggle. Cold Canadian fronts are clashing with warm moist air from the Gulf. The wind is blowing fiercely from alternating directions. Temperatures shift. Trees bend one way and then the other. Clouds race and swirl.

All these competing sensations come to focus in my belly — as fear and dread.

Doing all there really is to do, I let myself open mentally and physically to the whole of the turbulence, surrendering to what is. Looking up, I see that despite these strong currents, the billowing dark and white clouds, the sky remains blue, its clarity apparent through all else.

But then something else catches my attention: large birds, hawks, to keep from being battered by the competing forces, are cruising with wings held still, spiraling higher and higher within the updrafts created by the colliding fronts. They are not struggling, not avoiding, escaping, or collapsing, not even just coping, but are, instead, apparently delighting in the experience!

The tension in my body releases; fear and dread, the angst in my belly,

turn to joy. In the midst of distress, actually in openness to it, in this present
moment, anxiety becomes exhilaration.

    I am free.

— Personal retreat experience, October 2001

Momentary freedom is this simple. And any moment of freedom
can turn everything around, casting all of life's experiences in a new
light. Escape from times of struggle is not the final goal of spiritual
practice, nor is momentary freedom. However, every taste of the great
potentiality conditions the next, creating the possibility of further
experiential insights. With each opening comes not only freedom from
suffering but also greater ability to live responsibly and heartfully,
rather than reactively. Each such opening creates the likelihood of more
moments of opportunity and awakening. This experience of freedom is
simple, yet deeply profound. It is a living example of the opportunity
that may be available to us at any moment, the space from which a wise
and compassionate heart can naturally arise. To learn to intentionally
make small surrenders without compromising personal integrity is the
way to transform human consciousness, to come to realize what is true
and real, to live every moment as prayer.

Transformational experiences are always at hand, requiring only a
reorientation, a surrendering of ego control in any moment, letting go
of a solid sense of self and of identification with experience as I, me, or
mine. We let go, without collapsing. We learn to hold the discomfort of
even small and immediate losses. We come to awareness and acceptance
of the changing nature of things.

The initial experience of holding and surrender may feel like
suffering as the ordinary mind struggles for resolution, but the ability to
stay open to our entire experience with mindful awareness and not allow
the ego to preemptively dissipate the discomfort results not only in the
ending of suffering, but also the arising of ease of being, vitality, joy, and
greater freedom to love!

These are moments of realization, of knowing, and of being the kingdom now. Though we cannot produce mystical states or unitive experiences on command, we can intentionally foster circumstances that open us to contact with gifts of grace and to the great unity and connectedness that already exist. We do this through our choices, even in simple daily occurrences and momentary events. We learn to create a holding, an open-hearted acceptance of all experience, rather than escaping or contracting. We learn to be fully present to what is — surrendering to life just as it is.

Surrendering is quite different from collapsing or giving up. In fact, in giving up, the gestational holding does not occur. With adequate holding, faith and trust remain and flourish. Fear evaporates. Our personal and limited agendas come undone. We open and soften. We create space for something new — or very old, for that which is most true.

The transformation may actually be easiest to do in our most difficult situations, when the only thing we can do is surrender. Through challenging or desperate circumstances, we can come to understand how to release our habits of mind, our viewpoints, our positions or agendas. We learn and practice skillful means and then, in even the most ordinary daily events, we make surrender and ease of being a way of life.

Transforming consciousness may seem like a bold, even impossible, thing to do, maybe even New Age, but the topic has been responsibly addressed by many respectable sources.[1] It may also seem a difficult thing to talk about, but this is not really the case if we accept the limitations of the medium of language. Language can only point to the truth of our experience. The words and concepts themselves are not the truth, nor do they become the truth. All we can really understand is what we know in this moment through our direct experience, not through what we have been told, what we have read, or what we think.

I've been told, for example, many things about God. Some of the statements have been very useful, especially in desperate or fearful times, but my experience of God is what I trust most, though it seldom unfolds as I expect. The experience is vital and alive, in no way static. I no longer go where I want to go, carelessly or anxiously choosing my path. Instead, I am drawn into ways I never expected, many times consciously making choices, but with my heart/mind or an intuitive knowing, rather than with the logical mind. The result has been a journey into greater joy, fulfillment, and adventure than I could have ever conceived of or found through predetermined or linear processes. I always take what I've learned to my spiritual guides, Christian, Buddhist, and secular, to let them challenge my understanding, but the experience is my truest and most reliable resource.

The pointing out done through language and the teaching of various traditions, including this writing, are valuable in that they provide culturally specific ways to come to understanding. They create opportunities to share and foster an experiential grasp of what is true. But it is important not to confuse the pointing with the actual experience.

The experience we open to is the knowing that arises beyond or beneath our gift of language through our direct experience, as an interconnected, constantly changing organism, from physical sensations or states of mind and heart, qualities arising from within our immediate experience, information from all our senses, including the mind — the heart/mind.[2]

The understanding of heart/mind as consciousness is bigger than what we usually consider mind to be. Besides the usual teachings and definitions of mind, it includes qualities of mind and heart, emotions, feeling tones, sensual and kinesthetic information, processes, and our relationship to all of these. The meaning of consciousness can even expand further to include spaciousness or emptiness, the context from which everything arises.

What we don't experience directly, that is, what is separated to some degree or another from our direct experience, is conceptual. Though our ability to conceptualize is an indispensable skill, it is at least one step removed from our direct experience and therefore only hypothetically true.

In fact, everything we know is mediated by mind, so everything could be considered conceptual, even physical experience. Nevertheless, the experiences of body are a more direct and reliable resource for accessing reality; language and abstract thinking are helpful but not so reliable. Abstractions help us understand, but can also create greater and greater levels of separation from direct experience.

In a way, our sense information can actually provide a road map for our unfolding. When there is disagreement between the thinking mind and the instinctual or bodily self, the instinctual is more reliable for knowing what is true, though not necessarily more reliable for knowing how to respond. Through mindful attention to sense data, conceptual layers and habitual responses begin to fall away, getting us to direct experience free of our assumptions and conditioning.

A primary gift of Buddhist practices is to help us mature into trusting this expanded understanding and experience of mind or of consciousness, especially when it opens to aspects of experience that have otherwise been trumped by language, keeping us out of touch with immediate experience. In theistic terms, this means that we can have a direct experience of Mystery or of God, an experience involving the whole self, not just a mental event.

In working with heart/mind, it is helpful to think of consciousness as having two primary aspects and also as being a mediating experience of the two. Though delineation of the two aspects is helpful in discussion, the separation is not ultimately true. What may be most true is the mutually inclusive mediating space accessed when we learn to accept things as they are and when we are able to hold the tension of apparent dichotomies.

These two views of mind[3] and mediating space are the underlying concepts and the subject of exploration in this book. An overview of these concepts as I will use them follows.

Some approaches within Buddhist philosophy of what appear at first to be a delineated view of mind and reality include: conditioned-unconditioned, conventional-ultimate, relative-absolute, and the teachings of dependent arising (or dependent co-arising) and emptiness. In Christian terms we might use: branches-vine, or ego mind-God mind, though those terms bring into play a discussion I'm not prepared to address in detail here: without the vine there are no branches, but without branches is there no vine? The answer in the Christian tradition might posit that the context, the vine, the unconditioned, exists without the opposite of the pair, but without the other it wouldn't be manifested. In Buddhism it is understood that they are not separate. Form is emptiness,

emptiness is form. Everything is contained by emptiness, and emptiness manifests in all conditioned things.

I will mostly use the terms *ground consciousness* and *ordinary mind* in referring to these two views of mind because I find them less culturally loaded than others. I will also introduce the phrase *mediating space*. Using these terms has proven valuable, because I work in secular settings and among people from varied traditions.

A few words or names specifically referring to what I am calling *ground consciousness*, in addition to those mentioned above (unconditioned, ultimate, emptiness, vine, and God mind), include fullness, potentiality, deathlessness, silence, stillness, void, rigpa,[4] Mystery, Great Completion, or even God (if not a false image of God and if not limited to or less than immediate experience). *Ground consciousness* is really all-inclusive. It does not refer to something like a bottom line, but to a multidimensional field, boundaryless and timeless, that has a quality of aliveness, of vibrancy and vitality. Nothing is separate from it; everything arises from within it.

Ordinary mind, on the other hand, is part of and emanates from within ground consciousness and could be thought of as ego, ego mind, personality, linear mind, or conditioned mind. It includes all our ordinary human experiences and our conditioned relationships to these experiences, which may appear constant, but are actually in continuous flux and in continuous flow within and as a part of the ground consciousness. Ordinary mind is the primary consciousness we use to navigate in the world.

Between and including ground consciousness and ordinary mind is *mediating space*. Mediating space can be any time or place that rests neither on one side or the other of any dichotomy. It is timeless moments between everything past and everything future, the time or space between the vastness of the universe and the ground of earth, even the meeting of light and gravity.

Being between and within concrete and mystical, mediating space fits one interpretation of the Christian spiritual developmental stage of illumination, a stage of connection and fullness, but also emptiness. Its qualities are both sweet and tender and include simultaneous awareness and contentment combined with longing. Mediating space may also be considered to be experiences of liminal space referred to by the popular Christian teacher Richard Rohr.[5]

In summary, consciousness, including ordinary mind, ground consciousness, and meditating space, can be understood as being much bigger than what we normally think of as mind. Consciousness, according to the definition I am using, includes mechanisms of mind, brain, and body, and also all our experience and concepts. It includes sensual consciousness, that is, direct experience from all sense doors, including the mind as thought, but is not limited to these. It refers also to the context of things, the field from which all arises.

To come to the self-knowledge that Catholic saints and Christian mystics frequently speak of involves experiential familiarity with all aspects of consciousness, with both sides of these two ways of viewing mind, ordinary mind and ground consciousness, conditioned and unconditioned, as well as the mediating space. It includes all aspects of our limitations and of our vastness. This kind of understanding cannot come merely through reading; it requires mindfulness and investigation. Many exploratory road maps exist in teachings of the Buddhist path, some short and immediate, others gradual, as in the Christian understanding of the roads to Damascus and Emmaus.

In these discussions and in experiential investigations of transformational process, it is important neither to demonize the ego nor to understand it as isolated and separate. The ego has been extremely helpful in getting us through life to this point. It is the way we make sense of this worldly experience within a space/time continuum. More importantly, it is a great gift, the rare and human opportunity to flourish into fullness, the potentiality for manifesting the deepest reality in ordinary life.

∞

I offer here in three chapters some ways you might make such transformations, moving from direct and immediate to those that are more gradual and then to more and more intensive. I have included some basic practices in each chapter to ground and enhance your exploration. As you will see as you work with the resources offered in the bibliographies, the quantity of material available for working with heart qualities or wholesome mind states is immense.

Though some practices offered here are intended for explicitly working with heart qualities or wholesome mind states, most are tools to bring us back again and again to simple truth, to the beauty of knowing what is true and being free, to realization, to seeing and being the kingdom now. This is space in which we can get out of our own way and open to a natural radiance of heart. Ideally and ultimately, the simplest practices, the basic practices, are all that we really need; they are the place to start and the place to end.

In chapter 2 we look at knowing the heart/mind. We come to a direct experience of the fullness, breadth, and depth of consciousness, particularly to the insubstantiality of existence, as we understand it. This experience of mind or consciousness and self as basically lacking in substantiality or solidity is congruent with current scientific indications that the smallest particles of matter are unfindable.[6]

The idea of lack of substantiality may seem threatening or nihilistic. However, when we look closely at mind, we find that what we ordinarily think of as mind is ego or linear mind and is based on our identification with experience as I, me, or mine. Experientially, we can find more inclusive and more profound aspects of consciousness. When we get past the initial fear that this new perspective engenders, we begin to see the vast potential we may have been missing — and a great optimism arises.

Consciousness and human existence are more spectacular than we have come to believe. We find that we can impact our own experience in ways we had not conceived of. Change is not only possible; it is inevitable, and it is good news. Though we can't stop the flow, we can impact it; we can intentionally and skillfully participate. We can respond consciously and compassionately, rather than reactively.

Besides recognizing insubstantiality, we also come to appreciate and embrace our physical experience. I am proposing here that the body be used as the locus of spiritual practice, focusing exploration of spiritual work in and through physicality. Such focus is foundational in the ancient teaching of many cultures and is currently supported by scientific investigations demonstrating that the mind and body are not separate.[7] In Buddhist meditation practice, this connection is one of the first insights to arise. There is body and its manifestations, and there is mind in relationship to these events. Mind and body each influence and are influenced by the other.

Through direct awareness of our very bodies, we can come to an experiential grasp of even the most sophisticated theology or philosophy and into contact with our radiance of heart.

As our experiential understanding through mindful attention begins a deconstructive process in our misguided conception of mind, we begin to take ourselves less seriously. We open to deeper and broader understanding; we come to freeing the mind (chapter 3). This freedom brings us in touch with a powerful unity and flow in which we can participate actively by being dynamically still — or by being aware of or in contact with stillness in all actions.

In freeing the mind we intercede in the ordinary mind's processes in order to find release from hindrances of mind or unwholesome qualities of mind and from suffering. We open to joy, beauty, kindness, compassion, and freedom. Spiritual practice unveils powerfully wholesome qualities that naturally arise through simple mindful awareness and through skill in "getting out of the way" as ordinary mind lets go.

The model of the human brain as computer may no longer be sufficient.[8] In recent years we have found that the brain has the capability of restructuring itself. The brain does not stop developing, but adapts and grows.[9] It can work holistically[10] as well as linearly, often circumventing apparent limitation, sometimes even from physical damage. Unlike the workings of a computer, what comes out is not completely determined by what goes in! And the mind can actually change the brain.[11]

This restructuring can be done intentionally through prayer, particularly through meditation skills. We do so through volitional interventions, participating in kinds of meditation that incorporate body, mind, and heart. We employ practices of meditation or prayer that are not passive but dynamic and receptive.

When knowing the mind and freedom do not come easily or when noble heart qualities do not arise spontaneously, there are specific tools, precise treatments, for working with the challenge of opening to qualities of mind that may be especially difficult or stubborn. Through use of such tools we open ordinary mind with both kindness and great gentleness to more spaciousness, thus transforming awareness and consciousness. Applying these practices in intentionally shaping the mind, ordinary mind, is addressed in chapter 4.[12]

All are powerful embodied ways to pray.

Preliminary Attitudes
in Exploring Consciousness

Self-kindness is an essential first quality. This work is like no other in our culture. We are not generally prepared to learn and grow by being still, by not doing. The first rule of thumb in any activity (or non-activity) is asking if you are being kind to yourself.

If it is difficult to be kind to yourself, consider first if in the same situation kindness would be appropriate for someone else, especially someone dearly loved and precious to you — a child or a parent, a teacher or partner, a loved one.

Courage is required — courage to face everything that arises with openness and honesty, to be hungry for the truth, to choose to not get lost in self-judgment or ruminations.

The work also requires a willingness to let go, a willingness to be surprised, to open to the possible insubstantiality of everything we thought to be true, a willingness to suspend both belief and disbelief.

Preliminary Practices
in Exploring Consciousness

Be ready to ask yourself over and over again during life experiences: Is this really true? Is this really the way things are? Is my perspective correct? Do I have the whole picture?

Also, establish yourself in a life of simple integrity and ethical soundness. In Buddhist practice this ethical way of being can be summarized in the precepts stated very simply below. These are not rules to follow. They may look like Commandments, but are really more like the Sermon on the Mount. They are invitations to non-harming and to seeing, through direct experience, what causes harm and what brings peace, ease, and healing.

Refrain from taking what isn't freely given. Consider being generous.

Refrain from harmful or useless speech. Speak kindly and skillfully.

Refrain from sexual misconduct. Treat others and other relationships with respect.

Refrain from killing. Protect and respect all life.

Refrain from use of intoxicants or mind-altering substances. Maintain a clear mind.

Exploring the meaning of the precepts in lived experience is a strong foundation of spiritual practice. You will discover that as you work with consciousness and direct experience, evolving in your understanding and way of being, the precepts become not practices to maintain, but a most natural way of being. They become our way of life, because we have practiced them, because they are naturally the way of human happiness, and because they are within our innate capacity, in harmony with what is fundamentally true. An ease and peace come in living from this place of simple integrity.

Work with precepts by selecting one to relate to for a period of time, from a day to a month. Then within your life experience, notice your relationship to the precept, remembering that it is not a rule to follow, but an invitation to investigate or explore.

What does it mean to you? How skillful are you in the area? Is there a way to be with each precept that will make your life simple and happier? In what way can the precept help you be more at ease in life?

Another way to look at ethical behavior is in the teaching of the Eightfold Path, made up of three primary components: Ethics, Concentration, and Wisdom. The Ethics component includes Right Speech (one of the precepts), Right Livelihood, and Right Action (the precepts in general). Consider the challenging practice of applying observation as recommended above to the way you make a living and the way you invest money and other resources.

Recommended Reading in Consciousness

Abram, David. *The Spell of the Sensuous: Perception and Language in a More-Than-Human World.*

Cardenal, Ernesto. *Abide in Love.*

Culligan, Kevin, OCD, and Regis Jordan, OCD, eds. *Carmel and Contemplation: Transforming Human Consciousness.*

Dalai Lama. *Transforming the Mind: Teachings on Generating Compassion.*

Goleman, Daniel. *Destructive Emotions: How Can We Overcome Them? A Scientific Dialogue with the Dalai Lama.*

Kabat-Zinn, Jon. *Full Catastrophe Living: Using the Wisdom of Your Body and Mind to Face Stress, Pain, and Illness.*

Levine, Peter. *Waking the Tiger: Healing Trauma: The Innate Capacity to Transform Overwhelming Experiences.*

Shah, Idries. *Learning How to Learn: Psychology and Spirituality in the Sufi Way.*

Sumedho, Ajahn. *The Way It Is.*

Welwood, John. *Toward a Psychology of Awakening: Buddhism, Psychotherapy, and the Path of Personal and Spiritual Transformation.*

Wilber, Ken, Jack Engler, and Daniel P. Brown. *Transformations of Consciousness: Conventional and Contemplative Perspectives on Development.*

CHAPTER TWO

Knowing the Mind

The deepest level of communication is not communication,
but communion. It is wordless. It is beyond words. . . .
It is beyond speech, and it is beyond concept. . . .

We are already one, but we imagine we are not.
And what we have to recover is our original unity.
What we have to be is what we are.

—Thomas Merton

The most direct way to transform consciousness is simply to recognize and experience this heart/mind, to become familiar with it in all its manifestations and in its limitless potential. We come to experiential understanding of the all-inclusive nature of consciousness by first becoming familiar with the body and then developing intimacy with all its experiences and the relationships of the experiences. Through this awareness, based in the senses, we can actually come to direct knowledge of even the most sophisticated philosophical and theological teachings. Through simply becoming directly aware of our body/mind experience, we discover freedom, not as an idea but as direct experience. We discover freedom to see through the illusion of things.

Notice the way your body feels right now. Be aware of physical contact with the chair and the air surrounding you. Notice sensations in the body, qualities of denseness or lightness, fluidity or rigidity, temperature differences, and qualities of heart and mind that are all present and part of this current moment. You might even use the experience of reading this chapter as an opportunity and challenge to investigate the whole of your experience as you read, staying with the physical sensations, with the space, holding the text, and noticing resonations in the heart and body.

Try a little experiment right now. After reading this paragraph, close your eyes and bring attention to your experience of being a body, or as Anne Klein might say, "be your body from the inside." Investigate from within. By scanning the body as a whole and turning attention to its parts you might notice places of hardness or contraction, empty spaces and soft places, locations where the body is relaxed and open. Then focus attention on your hands, noticing whatever sensations are present there. Still with eyes closed, see if you can feel a clear line separating your hand from the surrounding air.

This is an uncomplicated, yet potentially powerful experience. You may not be used to scanning the body; in fact, we have often been discouraged from paying attention to feeling our bodies at all. We have been overtly taught through culture and religion to ignore bodily sensations as a protection from their "dangers." The result is that we've been a little afraid of our physical selves, our animal body, lacking confidence in our ability to not be dominated by sensation. Unfortunately, in our fear of being overtaken by sense desire, the desire and craving actually grow without our awareness. Skillful attention helps us meet felt needs instead of being unconsciously driven by them.

We have also become separated from our bodies because of our great involvement with concepts, mental processes, and our ability to think abstractly. Our gift of being able to read, write, and communicate verbally has replaced other kinds of knowing and communicating. In this enthusiasm for thought, we have lost touch with more direct and more subtle means of knowing and relating.

No matter what your level of body awareness, in doing the exercise above you may not have noticed a clear separation between hand and air. This is not because you should be able to feel such a split. In fact, trying to sense a division may be like trying to see the boundary lines of states or countries as drawn on maps, compared with our experience of the actual physical places. The boundary lines are useful for designation of entity, but aren't ultimately true. We can see the separation, but when sensually aware, we may not feel it. The lack of physical separation may be truer than the separation our mind believes to be true.

The body and the space surrounding it aren't totally separate. Consider our scientific knowledge that atoms and molecules are mostly empty space — and our developing understanding that the smallest particles of matter are unfindable. Isn't it logical that the separation is not a clear sharp line — and that possibly no line exists at all?

Further, by closing our eyes, as we often do in prayer or meditation, we close off the visual clues that separate us into apparently autonomous and self-sustaining entities, disconnected from one another. We find that our experience, learned from interaction of brain, senses, and environment, is in constant flux and flow, rather than being stable or formed. We may discover, instead, in the silence, the context out of which all other things arise, a pervasive stillness, a sense of potentiality or of spaciousness. In so doing, we overturn the understanding of what we take ourselves and the world to be.

In *An Anthropologist on Mars*, neurologist Oliver Sacks[1] tells stories of real people with brain disorders. In one chapter, Sacks describes a man who is given sight after being blind since early childhood. His first vision of the doctor's face is not that of a discrete entity, but rather a mere blur of color. This longtime sightless man had not yet *learned* to discriminate shapes, bodies, or faces from the visual field. How can we not wonder if perhaps he was seeing more purely?[2]

Ordinary Mind

What we usually think of as mind is our ordinary mind. The way Ayya Khema describes ordinary mind is quite simple and clear.

When we sit down to meditate, we are trying to transcend our everyday consciousness: the one with which we transact our ordinary business, the consciousness used in the world's market-place as we go shopping, bring up our children, work in an office or in our business, clean the house, check our bank statements, and all the rest of daily living. That kind of consciousness is known to everyone and without it we can't function. It is our survival consciousness and we need it for that. . . . our everyday consciousness is neither unique nor profound, it's just utilitarian.[3]

She goes on to say that this kind of consciousness is not deep enough to reach the breadth of who we are. It can't get to the most profound truths. But we can reach this deeper consciousness through meditation. "Meditation is therefore a means and not an end in itself. It is a means to change the mind's capacity in such a way that we can see entirely different realities from the ones we are used to."[4]

Through practices of meditation, particularly mindfulness meditation and openness to insight, this description of ordinary mind will expand to include awareness of all the sense doors and sense organs as well as the thinking mind. Ordinary mind can also include all thoughts and images of the thinking mind, as well as feeling tones, emotions, and states or qualities of mind.

After we've come in contact with these multiple aspects of ordinary mind and begin to clearly discriminate them in our experience, a deconstructive process comes into play. We discover unsatisfactoriness in all our grasping and wanting. We realize all is constantly changing. There is nothing to cling to. Nothing we cling to lasts. We come to an experiential understanding of the insubstantiality or emptiness of all phenomena. Our understanding of self as substantially existing is undone. All is movement — flux and flow and interconnectedness. Both sorrow and satisfaction change or disappear. As we recognize this, the ground consciousness, or greater mind, can shine through. The great potentiality opens for anything to happen, for change and for new possibilities — including wisdom, insight, and grace.

Basic Meditation Practice:
Insight and Mindfulness

Insight and mindfulness[5] include practices of coming to know through direct contact with current experience, by being grounded in physicality and open to awareness of the context of spaciousness or emptiness.

We begin the practice with eyes closed, sitting in a still, stable posture. After settling into the experience of being a body, being aware of being a body, and being aware of spaciousness and stillness, we turn attention to the breath. We let the breath become our primary meditation object, but remain open to space and to all bodily experience, neither shutting out events nor striving to be in touch with them.

After stabilizing attention at an anchor point in the breath, we open our focus enough to bring bare attention (a practice of being present to what is without overlay of concepts, unmediated by language or conceptualizations) to experiences that arise through the various sense doors. The sense doors include what we usually think of as the senses and the organs that are involved (eye and seeing, ear and hearing, nose and smelling, tongue and tasting, skin and feeling), but also the thinking mind.

The anchor of the breath remains a constant home for our attention. Whenever attention is lost or mind wanders aimlessly, we kindly and gently return attention to this anchor point. We steady the mind and again open to arising experience, staying attentive to predominant direct experience in all moments. First we do so in the formal sitting, then in any posture and any physical activity, beginning with walking, but eventually including all movement, at any time of day, and in any activity.

With time, continuing practice, mindfulness, and awareness of the still ground of consciousness, we may become aware of the mind's processes and its more subtle qualities, such as tightness or looseness. We also recognize how the mind instantaneously grasps for objects at various sense doors, reacts aversively to objects and experience, or even exhibits blindness — confusion or ignorance, in Buddhist terms. We may notice, as well, particular conditioned and pervasive qualities of mind and the changing nature of all experience.

We can play with our quality of attention and the choice of objects of attention, and then work with mindful awareness of unfolding processes. With time and attention to the present, we become aware of experiences from sense doors with gradually increasing clarity: well after experiences have arisen, as they are arising, or as they are about to arise. We become aware of the expectation of arising qualities and also know when the mind is strong enough that distractions will not appear.

All of this awareness is a kind of coming to know the "mind" and an awareness that challenges who we think we are. We begin to recognize our component parts, our animal-based physicality, our automatic responses, our incessant thinking, and our hidden or unobserved emotions. This process brings us to awareness of insubstantiality and prepares us to open to what is more true — our connectedness, the web of life — and what doesn't change, what is lasting: the constant flux or flow of greater mind, or ground consciousness, which is everything, including all of our experience.

To experience a taste of this greater mind, we can do a figure ground shift with our attention. Instead of focusing on the various objects that arise in our experience, we attend to the space around and containing them. This space can be considered a field of consciousness or the ground consciousness. It is space from which all events or objects unfold into existence, the fullness or ground from which all arises. In connecting with this space, which is the context of all experience, we lose a sense of separation. We may even feel one with this boundless consciousness.

Objects are part of this great space, interpenetrating it — not separate from the ground consciousness, but manifestations of it — so in using language and description, we are creating a dichotomy that does not ultimately exist. We can think of the objects instead as one with the ground, like waves in the ocean, or like particles or waves in physics, arising from and within the implicate[6] order of matter and energy,[7] static or flowing. More simply, what arises appears, depending upon our way of thinking about it, like looking at life events in terms of nouns or verbs, as objects or processes. We may also be aware of surface structure, but oblivious to deep structure — aware of manifestations of objects, thoughts, or events, rather than seeing a deeper meaning undergirding what is readily apparent.

Ground Consciousness

Coming to recognize this ground consciousness is a foundational experience of most spiritual practices. I am using the term to include any conceptions of consciousness beyond the mechanistic thought created through functioning of the human brain. In fact, conceptualizations are important in this process, but can only point to the knowing that is accessed through direct experience. I think of it as ground consciousness, not because it is solid or basic like earth, but because it is a vast field that contains everything and is everything. Ground consciousness, as I am using the term, is the context in which all content is embedded or from which all content unfolds.

Though ground consciousness itself is constant and unchanging, it is a fluid constant, manifesting continually in various forms. Ironically, what is most constant is its lack of constancy, its changeability. All phenomena are part of it, arise from within it, and fold back into it.[8]

The Dalai Lama describes what I am referring to as ground consciousness as follows:

> With persistent practice, consciousness may eventually be perceived or felt as an entity of mere luminosity and knowing, to which anything is capable of appearing and which, when appropriate conditions arise, can be generated in the image of whatsoever object. As long as the mind does not encounter the external circumstance of conceptuality, it will abide empty without anything appearing in it, like clear water. Its very entity is that of mere experience. Let the mind flow of its own accord without conceptual overlay. Let the mind rest in its natural state, and observe it. . . . in time the mind appears like clear water.[9]

We can think of this ground consciousness as consisting of clarity and knowing.[10]

Clarity can be accessed through meditative practices of concentration and mindful awareness. In concentration we steady the mind. This is done in meditation by initially focusing attention closely on one object. The possible objects are many — the breath, a word, a chant, or a visual image, to name only some of the most common. Concentration practices still the mind by giving it an alternative focus. This focus helps bring the mind to rest, to stopping, to relief, to freedom. The steady mind comes to various degrees of openness: from stillness, to spaciousness, to clarity, and even to "luminosity," as mentioned above by the Dalai Lama.

The breath is especially valuable as a concentration tool for several reasons. It is easily accessible and can be used at any time in any circumstance. The breath is content-neutral, yet has spiritual connotations in virtually every tradition. More importantly, attention to the breath centers concentration on the body, creating the possibility of coming into direct contact with experience. In fact, through attention to breath, we can facilitate awareness emanating from the body itself, knowing that could be defined as proprioceptive — involving the whole body through all the senses, "the ability to sense the position, location, and movement of the body and its parts."[11]

Breath as a meditation object is even more important when considering the second aspect of ground consciousness, that of knowing. Knowing is predicated on the clarity of concentration (and is equally as important as clarity). We come to knowing, to insight, through lucid, mindful observation of our experiences — at first as object and then from the subjective mode, from within the experiences.

Observing objectively from outside the experiences, we create the possibility of letting go of identification with our ordinary experience of self, our embeddedness in events, and our automatic unconscious responses. Having thus moved to a place of relative detachment, we are able to participate with conscious subjectivity, consciously observing from within experiences. In the process we come to know ourselves as breath as we observe the breath; we are body as we are aware of its experiences. We relate to our physical experience from the inside, not as a bystander (though the bystander role is a natural step in the process), not visualizing or seeing what our experience is, but being the experience and holding it in the spaciousness of emptiness or clarity of consciousness. Objects become flows, or dynamism, that are not separate from, but one with, experience.

Breath has an added benefit in this exploration because of its fluid nature and because of its lack of permanence and simultaneous constancy or reliability. As with life and life experiences, we can influence the breath but not completely control it. It repeatedly arises and passes away.

Because the foundation is clarity and spaciousness, there is possibility for flow within the ground consciousness. Change is possible. Without this space there would be only one object, no separation, no flow, and no potentiality — only death.

The ground consciousness is also not void, as in neutral or indifferent. It can be depicted as the source, the base of any wholesome quality of mind. In fact, there are Buddhist scriptures that delineate the natural arising of these wholesome qualities as we break through spirals of illusion.[12]

When we break through, when we simply stop and let compulsive thought subside, wholesome qualities arise, often in predictable sequence — first faith, then joy, to even greater qualities of sublime contentment. Compassion arises. We stop creating the suffering that results from unnecessary struggles against the way things are.

Every time we have such a release to freedom from suffering, a quality of faith deepens. The faith supports further our ability to stay with future experience and be transformed by the process.

Often experiencing clarity is enough to get a taste of freedom of being. We become unencumbered from negativity of all kinds, from heavy mind states and emotions. Our relationship to physical pain changes and may actually decrease.[13] With clarity we begin to experience lightness.

A natural benefit of any conscious or mindful moment is simply pleasurable interest, a result of being in touch with what is real. We develop a natural comfort in living with the body and a sense of being deeply at ease in all circumstances of life.

Of course, this does not always and spontaneously occur. It is also not a one-time event. Rather, this sudden opening, this rotation in perspective, must be recognized and accepted again and again. A great gift of meditation practice is that it provides the tools for exploration and investigation and the increasing capability of implementing them. These are tools for the journey of discovery that make it possible for us to actually make the choices.

Beginning Practice
for Knowing the Mind

Begin to notice the difference between direct contact with experience from any or all sense doors (eyes, ears, nose, tongue, skin, and thinking mind) and thoughts about those events. That is to say, notice the difference between direct experience or bare attention and mental elaborations, concepts, or conceptualizations that follow the direct contact.

Choose to do this exploration whether or not you really understand the exercise. It is designed to help you begin discovery of unmediated experience, direct contact with the current moment's experience.

An activity that might include opportunity to explore experiences of all sense doors is eating. Pay close attention to the breadth of experience during a meal or even in consuming just one morsel — a nut, candy, or a piece of dried fruit. Approach the food as a fresh new experience — as if you had never been exposed to it.

Recommended Reading for Knowing the Mind

Bohm, David. *Wholeness and the Implicate Order.*

DeCharms, Christopher. *Two Views of Mind: Abhidharma and Brain Science.*

Macy, Joanna. *Mutual Causality in Buddhism and General Systems Theory: The Dharma of Natural Systems.*

Sacks, Oliver. *An Anthropologist on Mars: Seven Paradoxical Tales.*

———. *The Man Who Mistook His Wife for a Hat: And Other Clinical Tales.*

Salzberg, Sharon. *Faith: Trusting Your Own Deepest Experience.*

Talbot, Michael. *The Holographic Universe.*

Zajonc, Arthur, ed. *The New Physics and Cosmology: Dialogues with the Dalai Lama.*

CHAPTER THREE

Freeing the Mind

*When the mind is still, tranquil, not seeking
any answer or any solution, neither resisting
nor avoiding — it is only then that there can be
a regeneration, because then the mind is capable
of perceiving what is true; and it is truth that
liberates, not your effort to be free.*

—J. KRISHNAMURTI

James Hollis, a Jungian analyst, gave a talk at the Houston Jung Center when he became its director in 1998. He said something at the time that astounded me in its implications. He said that one of his primary tasks was to depathologize anxiety.

I understood him to mean that it is the nature of the ego to be anxious. Anxiety is the natural ego response in the face of our evolutionary unfoldment. As we become free, it holds on tighter. Hollis suggested that the only thing to do when this happens is to let go and to move forward anyway, despite the anxiety, the fear produced by the ego.[1]

If we have already chosen a fundamentally ethical life, if we are living a moral life beyond legalism or need for rules and regulations, we can realize that this anxiety is a good sign, an indication that we may be moving toward freedom from the ego's domination, freedom to explore new realms and new ways of understanding. We find ourselves free to embark on the most fascinating and enticing journey of spiritual unfoldment.

When we go forward, there will continue to be resistance, but, quoting James Hollis, we just "put on our hip boots and keep wading," staying in touch with reality or truth of current circumstances without taking any of it too seriously. Resistance is just resistance. Eventually, we will move through the resistance and into ever-increasing moments of vitality and joy of being.

It is helpful in this process to remember that nothing is as substantial as it appears to be. There are other ways to relate, another way to identify ourselves. By being open to the truth of given circumstances and being in contact with spaciousness of mind, we learn to live on the cutting edge of our freedom and our safety. We become fully alive when we are awake between our past and our future. We live in the dynamic present. When we can live in this mediating space, in touch with both the spaciousness and our animal bodies, we are whole human beings.

To be consciously in the moment, we have to separate to some degree from the ego or ordinary mind, disidentifying and being able to observe our own experience before we can help ourselves in the process of evolving and manifesting our potential fullness and depth. The ego is not as important as it takes itself to be, but its power can stand in the way of our wholeness, freedom, and joy. It is ego's nature to get anxious when we begin to be free and fuller. Our task is to see the fear or anxiety directly and clearly — then to treat ourselves, in the experiencing of anxiety, firmly and gently, as we would handle a fearful child, and go forward in kindness.

Anxiety is the natural response of the ego to our opening to greater experience of what it is to be a human being. This ego response to growth often feels like fear. But if we can learn to be open to the fear, not identify with the experience as fear or suffering, but see it instead as a currently arising resistance to change, then we can move beyond its limitations. We let the action and the flow of life be our prayer.

Once we recognize our experience, we can free the mind through *volitional intervention*. When we learn the skill of intentionally intervening, we can live a life of *dynamic receptivity*. We can also *create* in the world without overt acting. We let skillful action arise by working with attention and intention, yet with little ego activity, participating with the body and/or personality.

There are other ways of creating. We may need to work with skillful energy to develop abilities, technical skills, and appropriate credentials, but we do not rely on heavy-handed ego intervention or self-flagellation to produce. With too much ego involvement, results do not flow naturally. We become owned by the process rather than dancing the process.

Beautiful and wholesome results come out of joy and flow and from great delight in exploration and discovery. With baseline skills that support our love and interest, and with release of need for preconceived and precise outcomes, creating can occur! The process can be joyful.

The easiest examples of moments of pure creating without ego activity may be in the performance of music, the arts, and in some athletics. Of course, effort is required to develop the skills for this kind of creating, but the art of creating is not in the effort. Actual art, art that is joyful and that reflects the transcendent, flows with skill but from a ground of freedom.

Volitional Intervention

Volitional intervention is a direct way to free the mind by recognizing what it is doing and just dropping dysfunctional thinking. This is easier said than done. Labeling experience as it arises is a useful tool. Labeling our experience may allow enough separation to see objectively.

We can do this by labeling events in the stream of experience. Most simply, when you notice thought or mental events, say silently and very softly to yourself *thinking*. When noticing sensations from sense doors other than the mind, note *sensing*. You may choose to name these events, or objects of attention, more specifically: in regard to mind or thinking you might use *past*, *future*, and *nonsense*; or *planning*, *remembering*, *hoping*, *wanting*. In regard to sensing, use *hearing*, *seeing*, *tasting*, *smelling*, *touching*. Do this only if you can do so without getting wrapped up in trying to decide which term to use. Note or name softly in the mind so that the experience remains primary. Think of it as whispering, silent whispering. Only about 5 percent of your attention is on the labeling or noting; 95 percent remains in contact with the experience.

Dropping dysfunctional thinking does not mean ignoring an experience or disassociating from it, though there is really not much chance of doing this. The process can be trusted; it has an intelligence of its own. What needs attention usually keeps demanding attention. If not recognized, it expresses itself by more and more persistent means. It is important neither to ignore the experience nor to respond reactively, but rather to address what needs attention.

It is helpful to face such demands as if they were those of a young child that one is responsible for and loves deeply. Of course one pays attention — but only as needed and when appropriate; then one turns back to personal tasks. Learning balance in this and other circumstances could be defined as the whole of spiritual practice. (This idea of balance involves all aspects of our experience and will be addressed further in chapter 4.)

There are various levels of this type of intervention. In a longtime formal meditation practice that is both diligent and disciplined, one can observe very subtle experience from various sense doors *arising*, having *arisen*, and *passing away*. In such a practice there is greater opportunity than in the busyness and multiplicity of daily life to notice automatic responses and intervene in the experience at quite discrete levels.

Even so, in well-supported formal practice, we will usually notice an experience only after it has arisen. Noticing well after experiences have arisen is even more likely in daily life, where the awareness processes, such as noticing anger or jealousy, are likely to operate at a more gross level, when they are already fully arisen and functioning. We often explore the experience in retrospect, looking back to see the way the processes were unfolding.

With skillful attention and mindfulness, we might be able to uncover the opportunity for intervention. An especially critical point arises within the unfolding of experience. There is an automatic movement that arises in response to, or even in conjunction with, information at the sense doors. These are amoebic-like reactions — immediate non-volitional responses to stimuli. These automatic responses are followed instantaneously by movements toward and movements away from experience. The automatic responses are subtle but highly influential feeling tones. It is helpful to develop the skill of noticing the feeling tones as early in the unfolding process as possible and to label them as *pleasant* or *unpleasant*. Moving toward objects suggests that a *pleasant* response has occurred, and moving away, an *unpleasant* response. Our response may also be *neutral* or *indifferent*.

At first we might consider a neutral response as *pleasant* simply because it is not unpleasant and we are not suffering because of it; however, in time, as our observation skills increase, we find it useful to begin noticing the difference between what is actually *pleasant* feeling and what is *neutral* or *indifferent*, what we may be shutting out or really not tuning in to.

These automatic responses are totally beyond our control, nonvolitional unfoldings. Unnoticed, they flow further along in process to become fully manifested mind states, qualities of mind, or emotions.

With precise observational skills, when some kind of discomfort triggers movement or intention toward unskillful action, we can learn to see it coming, even to know that certain circumstances are likely to bring the tendency into our range of experience. A skillful response is not to suppress the experience, the emotion, the mind state, the feeling tone, or the kinesthetic reverberations; but only to be fully present to the experience, to stop and consider whether action should be taken or not, to make contact with emptiness or insubstantiality, to rest in mediating space, to become a holding without reactivity.

An example of how this might unfold in formal meditation practice follows.

Something may be coming up that needs attention. At first I keep turning my attention elsewhere, generally to an anchor point in the body and breath, not sure that what is coming up isn't just a sideshow or mini soap opera ready to carry me away from the present moment. But it is persistent or popping up over and over, so I turn my attention toward the experience and more fully recognize its presence.

I may even name the experience, but if so, very loosely. Naming can reify an experience. This is definitely not the intent. I do want to be aware of what is happening. I merely whisper a name or general word in a possible category of the experience, not spending a lot of time defining. Simultaneously I recognize that the name is merely a conventional label to help the process.

I may also note the automatic arising of a felt sense and identify it as "pleasant," "unpleasant," or "indifferent." The felt sense may have already flourished into some degree of anger or fear, perhaps doubt or desire, or something subtler, like noticing pleasure, pleasantness, or attachment, maybe even attachment to an unhealthy quality or experience.

These may not be qualities I care to be associated with, but they are present, so I accept things just as they are. The distasteful quality of mind is arising or is fully present. I simply accept its presence, without judgment. I do not push it away, hang on to it, or pursue it.

In neither pushing away nor pursuing, in just allowing the truth to be, I create a holding for my conflicting experiences, whether they manifest as sensations, thought, feeling tones, or emotions. I stay with this experience, exploring it in various aspects: in how the body feels, in qualities of mind and heart that are present. Though at times intellectual involvement is certainly helpful and appropriate, I don't usually explore thoughts about the experience in my formal meditation practice. Thoughts can often add fuel to the fire ("fueling a fire" is actually an expression that the Buddha used to describe this experience).

The next thing I do is the opposite of eliminating or substituting. I choose to be interested in the experience. I explore it further, being especially aware of experiences in the body.

In this case, and this is often true, what I have not been willing to see is something I don't want to believe is true. But not wanting to believe or see doesn't change the circumstances; in fact, the seeing releases the hold it has on me. It also loses its apparent substantiality.

Truth is always freeing. And it is never as bad as we expect it to be. Carl Jung said that 90 or 95 percent of what we sublimate is pure gold.

These may also be experiences we haven't been willing to see. Further, there are experiences we have simply learned to tune out, as well as experiences that we never learned to recognize because they don't fit our understanding of how the world works.

Once I've investigated an experience (at whatever level is appropriate in the circumstance), I might be able to recognize the truth of the way things are, the insubstantiality of all I have taken to be so real, or I may choose not to identify with it. This ability to be free to choose or not choose is an important capacity, a capacity leading to a fuller freedom that comes from recognizing the nature of things. Whatever I am experiencing is part of the continual flow of change, phenomena rolling along. It does not define who I am. I remain responsible, but act only if action is required and when it is clear what skillful action is called for.

Dynamic Receptivity

In hard times I've always loved the blues. Some devastating event can occur, but through music I can connect with the universal threads of suffering. I realize that in suffering I am not alone or unique. I ride the blues through to the other side — to connectedness with all of humanity, all of life.

We can practice this intervention in daily life — recognizing mediating space and being a holding for dichotomies — for any difficult experience. I think of it as *dynamic receptivity* — the way meditation or receptive prayer moves from being passive to active.

Like a koan, life presents many opportunities to reside in mediating space, to practice this holding, to just be with our experience as it is, because there is so much we cannot control. A koan is used in some Zen schools to confound the mind, to bring the self in touch with the direct experience of both the conditioned and the unconditioned, the self and the not-self, the ego or personality and the spaciousness, and the release into freedom.

Life experiences that can squeeze us into freedom are similar to the mental challenges of koans. They may be paradoxes or experiential conundrums. Many times there may be a disconnect between two seemingly impossible circumstances or between how things are and how we'd like them to be. There are dilemmas, apparent contradictions, and impossible circumstances. The similarity between these challenges and koans is that they cannot be resolved by thinking — only through accepting things as they are and learning the patience to hold experience until there is understanding, freedom, and clarity about right action, including the possibility of no action at all.

Abiding in mediating space requires that we be aware of opposing movements and stay with them. We choose not to run away or take some other preemptive action. Instead, in creating a holding, we can make a space for insight to arise or, as stated in Christian terms, for grace to manifest. Of course, we can't control the outcomes, the grace, or the insight, but we can create the space. And we can influence the outcomes (see Unconstructed Creating later in this chapter).

Staying with the experience is a way of surrendering without shutting down or escaping. In making this a way to pray, we stay in touch with the suffering, especially through body awareness, sense contact, the dichotomies, whatever current reality is; but we let go of outcomes. We realize that the ego mind is not enough; the ego mind may have even brought us to this crossing. We hold the discomfort, letting it "cook." The struggle may just burn away. Sometimes grace or insight arises. Sometimes miraculously so.

Difficult situations force us into this holding, unless we prematurely remove ourselves with one of the plethora of numbing tools that our culture provides: drugs (including alcohol and prescription medications), books, work, sex, parties, games, studies, self-improvement, cosmetics, shopping . . . name yours.

The experience of being honest and open to the truth is much more satisfying than anything that has become one of our numbing tools. Choosing to stay with difficult and challenging experiences can bring us to the pleasure that accompanies simply being with the truth, a felt sense resulting from surrendering to things as they are. Buddhist teachings in some traditions include the understanding that by being mindfully present and focused, a quality may arise of simple pleasurable interest. The pleasure is not necessarily what we might usually think of as pleasurable, being more subtle than usual expectations (especially in an abundant society), yet, on the other hand, it may very well be a viscerally pleasurable experience.

Staying with experiences, being fully open and mindful, is the way to their unraveling or to our transforming — all in spite of us.

Committed relationships, either individual or communal, are powerful ways to intervene with ourselves. We maintain a holding in our commitments, supporting our ability to be dynamically receptive. This is important to do because any time we put ourselves into relationship with "other" we can come to a better understanding of ourselves. We can embrace a taste of the great richness in all the flavors of different human beings, different cultures, races, and gender. We can choose to let ourselves be seen and be influenced.

Personal relationships can bring us into very difficult and challenging places. Staying with these experiences and the processes involved, we come to the discovery, in lived experience, of a great paradox: in creating a holding for the suffering without getting lost or drowning in pain, the deepest experience of joy can manifest. This does not mean that suffering or pain is a requirement for joy. Holding with patience and with acceptance for the way things are is the essential element. It facilitates and supports personal integrity, a sense of well-being, and contentment. It changes our relationship to the circumstances, freeing us from their apparent substantiality.

Self-kindness is always a fundamental rule. The value of committed relationships is undercut when there is abuse or harm. If a committed relationship is life-depleting, then we need to consider carefully whether it is time to stay or leave. In such cases we may find that we are no longer committed to each other, but to an empty commitment. In any relationship, we can always choose to keep someone in our hearts without giving away our lives and our peace of mind. Just as all beings are precious, so are we!

Whenever possible, staying connected, heart-connected, with challenging experiences can reap the great benefits of holding or of waiting. We gain faith from seeing the effects in any situation, especially the most desperate. We have the confidence and appreciation that come from knowing we have done everything we can. This is the virtue of Christian *fortitude* or Buddhist *courageous effort*.

Eventually we start to intentionally use patient holding, abiding in mediating space, in day-to-day circumstances, surrendering the ego by choice in the smallest of matters, recognizing and accepting things as they are, and letting wise action arise or become evident.

We may also begin to use holding or access mediating space intentionally to help manifest our heart's greatest desires and create without effortful constructing or overt ego-directed activity.

Unconstructed Creating

We can choose to create by intentionally setting up and observing the dichotomy between reality and our deepest desires. We do this by staying in touch with current reality and simultaneously remembering these fundamental desires. One way of living life consistent with our hearts is to make this remembering a formal part of our day, including prayers of intention as part of a daily offering. (See Appendix A for samples of Buddhist and Christian prayers of intention.)

We may also take moments during the day to remember our heart's deepest intentions. Transition times are great opportunities to be still and let right action unfold. Even at this very moment, ask yourself: *What is the deepest calling in my life? What is it that motivates my most skillful actions?* Think back to the beginnings of your intentional spiritual path or revisit the motivations for the work you have in hand. By doing this for even just three to five minutes, you may create space for wise actions to arise. You may break free of the limitations of conditioned mind and access a great intrinsic shepherding force that supports your deepest heart desires.

We can create nobly and without busy doing only if we are not attached to outcomes. We may have general intentions, even specific intentions, but we remain free to learn and modify as we go. As we acquire additional information, experience and being awake make it possible for us to reorient ourselves and try something new, modifying our process and refining or clarifying our intentions.[2]

The potentiality of the next moment is totally unpredictable. Whatever occurs is a result of not just one thing or another, but of multiple causes and conditions. Causality is not linear. Everything occurs in relationship to everything else. The world is really very complex, but also reliable in its complexity.

Each action within our matrix of experience influences what follows for good or for ill. If we can remain open and faithful to our holding and our deepest heart's desire, then insights and skillful responses arise. Further, with each skillful action we condition the next moments to be wholesome, joyful, and constructive.

Being aware of continuous options and choosing skillful ones is a habit that develops, grows, and becomes easier with each *Yes* to what is most wholesome. Our intentions set the conditions for continued desirable outcomes.

When spontaneous wholesome behavior does not occur, we can choose to turn to practices that foster wholesome response, practicing openness to deep heart qualities. We address these in the following chapter.

Beginning Practices
for Freeing the Mind

Stay in contact with your body — catch yourself during the day being aware of breath or sense experiences. Notice being in contact with the chair or the ground, the air, and movement.

When you notice yourself feeling stressed, fearful, empty, or lonely, stay in physical contact with yourself rather than running away, escaping, or filling up the space with some distraction or other. You may find that what you are avoiding is something that may even be interesting, particularly fun, pleasurable, or important to you. Just say *Yes* to yourself. Give yourself permission to stay with the experience, to go forward. Take the risk!

❧◯◯❧

Waiting and transition times during the day (between one task and the next, at stop lights and in lines) are a great neutral time to start connecting with the body and breath. We can use natural breaks to create space for the possibility of surprise movements and choices that can radically change the day — even our whole life! Do this by just pausing and breathing. Be in touch with the body, the breath, and with immediate experience — simply knowing you are alive.

❧◯◯❧

Explore your deepest intentions. Give yourself moments in the day to revisit them.

❧◯◯❧

Make a note, *breathing*, whenever you notice breath during your day. Go to sleep gently riding the breath. In time you may even come to notice breath in your sleep. Pay attention to the first breath awareness of the day until attention to the breath becomes the way you wake up in the morning.

Select a sense door to work with for a day. Softly note any time you catch yourself *thinking, hearing, seeing, tasting, smelling, touching.*

Give yourself a meditation or prayer session and/or a whole day to note *pleasant, unpleasant,* and *neutral* or *indifferent.* See if you can notice these feeling tones as they arise and before they pervade experience, forming full-blown unskillful qualities of mind, before they move into judgments of liking or disliking experience or into grasping or aversion. You might also start with the strong emotions, tracing them back to the originating feeling tone.

Confront the reality of death. As monks and teachers from different traditions have advised, *live with death on your shoulder,* remembering that it is an ever-present possibility and the inevitable end of this life story for everyone. We don't know when it will happen or how, and easily forget that sooner or later our own embodied life will end, as will that of all our loved ones and all our enemies. We also don't know through our own experience what will follow.

Visit nursing homes or people that are ill. Become a hospice volunteer. Be present with friends who are sick or dying. Admit and accept your own aging body.

Observe the decomposition of an animal body as it occurs in natural life experience.

Intentionally open to ground consciousness, to spaciousness, to the context of things. Release your stories, both precious and horrendous, and rest in vast space and openness.

Choose a small safe place, five to ten paces long, to do a special walking practice. Walk back and forth on this short pathway, paying close attention to your feet making contact with the earth or to the flow of movement in your legs, feet, or body. Pay close attention to the physical experience and the movement. After some time, when you are comfortable and in contact with physicality, briefly close your eyes, remaining aware of the body movement, but also of the stillness. Perhaps you can become aware of both the body movement and the mind that does not move.[3]

∝◯◯◠

Recommended Reading for Freeing the Mind

Amaro, Ajahn. *Small Boat, Great Mountain: Theravadan Reflections on the Natural Great Perfection.*

Franck, Frederick. *Zen Seeing, Zen Drawing: Meditation in Action.*

Fritz, Robert. *The Path of Least Resistance: Learning to Become the Creative Force in Your Own Life.*

———. *Your Life as Art.*

Macy, Joanna. *Mutual Causality in Buddhism and General Systems Theory: The Dharma of Natural Systems.*

———. *World as Lover, World as Self.*

Norbu, Chogyal Namkhai. *Dzogchen: The Self-Perfected State.*

Smith, Rodney. *Lessons from the Dying.*

CHAPTER FOUR

Shaping the Mind

*No one ever imagines that self-observation may be
a highly disciplined skill, which requires longer training
than any other skills we know of.*

—JACOB NEEDLEMAN

When the ordinary mind is especially resistant to releasing some pattern that is too intense and ingrained to be let go, then we can work directly and intentionally with the ordinary mind. We work with this ordinary mind to gently shape it into harmony or correspondence with the wholeness of mind or with ground consciousness.

We have already explored some means for doing this. We first come to a realization of emptiness, the ground consciousness. Then we combine it with awareness of current experience and mindful attention to even the subtlest nuances of experience. This requires an ability and willingness to stay present, creating a holding for conflicts, abiding in mediating space.

We have noted that when we are attentive to our own experience as it arises, we can intervene with ourselves, *freeing* the mind through recognition of the way things are or through volitional intervention, which is possible because of our *knowing* through bare attention and mindfulness. We can structure our experiences by simply being clear about our intentions and being present to current reality.

When, despite all these practices, unwholesome mind states dominate our experience or when they are very painful, we turn, in kindness to ourself, to teachings, traditional and contemporary, intended for manifesting wholesome qualities of mind. We might also turn to these practices just to reconnect with the heart qualities, choosing to be increasingly conscious of wholesome qualities in our daily life.

Working with wholesome qualities is based on awareness and mindfulness. We establish ourselves in awareness of emptiness with mindfulness of all current experience, but particularly attend to qualities of mind, which ebb and flow like all other experience. The difference in mind qualities (as compared to phenomena already addressed) is their pervasiveness in our experience. One little event, even the subtlest sensory experience, can shift the whole mind into some enveloping quality or another. A mind quality is a gestalt-like experience. It is similar to the complete coloring of life that occurs when we are wearing tinted glasses, or like the color that permeates a whole piece of cloth when one corner is dipped in ink.

By recognizing these subtle and stubborn qualities of mind, we get in touch with our entire experience from the inside. We can recognize the gestalt that includes all of the present moment, not just awareness of the separate objects. This global awareness might be something like Eugene Gendlin's felt sense,[1] or Eckhart Tolle's pain body,[2] a coloring of the whole of who we are. It is bigger than the body, energetic, amorphous, and impermanent. The experience can take on a life of its own, only to fade away or be replaced with another.

We can easily miss these affective tones. We are generally deeply identified with them and thus are unable to see them. We also miss them by skipping directly to emptiness or by being busy with the content of experiences, stories, and isolated thoughts, or with discrete sensations, even by being too tightly focused on our meditation object, whether it be the breath, a word, or a phrase.

Balancing — Finding the Middle Way
(Dynamic Equilibrium)

The beginning point and opportunity for transformation occurs before these full-blown mind states arise, with awareness of the automatic response of *pleasant, unpleasant, neutral* or *indifferent*. Once noticed, we can be aware of the arising process and intervene, influencing and changing the progression of the experience. We can also form an intention to be more open in future moments to all experience in an increasingly equanimous mode of being. This intention conditions our response positively toward wholesome behavior in future experiences.

Of course, intervening is not easy to do. We are much more likely to catch ourselves in a formal meditation practice than in daily life. In daily life we are more likely to notice our experience only with a fully erupted mind state. But we can develop skill at early recognition. We can, at any point in the process, even in mid-sentence (literally or figuratively), recognize what is unfolding and make a conscious choice for a more skillful response.

A fundamental teaching of the Buddha, one that sets it apart from all others, is found in the teaching of the Four Noble Truths which states that the cause of suffering — ignorance of the nature of things as insubstantial and thus unable to provide lasting satisfaction — disappears when we stop or let go of clinging. More traditionally stated: there is suffering in life, but there are causes for suffering. When we recognize the causes, there is freedom from suffering. There is a noble path to follow.

This understanding can be viewed on different levels. If we can see the causes in the context of being aware of the empty or insubstantial nature of reality, we have sufficient wisdom to be free through insight alone. But on a more typical level, the mundane or ordinary level, when we are aware of causes, we can use various skillful means to become free from pain and unnecessary suffering.

Working mindfully with balance is an important part of this process, incorporating many skillful means. Among the most common and recognizable unwholesome or unskillful qualities of mind are restlessness or sluggishness, being too tight or too loose. Other common experiences are grasping or rejecting and reaching or averting. They can even show up in just leaning forward or leaning backward.

These qualities, which I have paired, are opposites and show up both mentally and physically. The mind will reflect the physical experience; the body will reflect what is happening in the mind. In working with the body and mind, and in clear sensing, we can learn to find balance between the extremes. Through working mindfully with balance, we can learn to live life in the body as if playing a musical instrument, neither flat nor sharp, neither too tight nor too loose.

When the body is in balance, the mind will follow (and vice versa). We live in acceptance and clarity of what is, with whatever qualities of mind arise. Rather than trying to escape or reject any experience, we can learn to work with skillful effort and skillful attention to stay in balance. The balance is not static, but dynamic — dynamic equilibrium. We fully participate, not withdrawing, but remaining in touch with life and the refuge of stillness.

Fostering Wholesome Qualities of Mind

When experiences are especially painful or when it is most difficult to find balance, it is helpful to turn to direct practices that illuminate our most basic characteristics of faith, love, and compassion. These exhilarating and joyful qualities are truer, more basic, to what we are than the unwholesome or unskillful qualities, which can be thought of as veils or obscurations.

Though compassion and wisdom are primary outcomes of Buddhist practices, loving-kindness is viewed — in Theravada Buddhism, at least — as the most fundamental wholesome quality to foster (within the context of the realization of emptiness and the development of mindfulness). Loving-kindness is also a component of all other wholesome mind states. Hence, practices of other qualities are sometimes lumped under the general heading of loving-kindness, or *metta* (a Pali word, the probable language of Gautama Buddha). Once we learn how to work with loving-kindness, we can easily apply both loving-kindness and its basic practices to other desirable qualities of mind, particularly, but not limited to, compassion, equanimity, and empathetic joy.

These practices do not always bring up the qualities we are inviting. Sometimes what comes forward instead is just the opposite, the qualities that are standing in the way of our openness and the flowering of wholesome qualities. But with formal practice and mindful attention, we more readily recognize them as they arise.

The most common introductions to loving-kindness come in the form of exercises or guided meditations that include well-wishing to self and others. These guided meditations may also refer to attention, energy, warmth, or light directed toward a variety of beings. Traditionally, mindful attention is aimed first at the self, then a benefactor, followed by a good friend, a neutral person, and a difficult person. Loving-kindness is then increasingly expanded from our individual selves to all sentient beings in the entire universe. In doing this practice, it is understood that we are fostering our own quality of being, not that of the other. Also, we are not creating new qualities or gaining something that was lost, but opening to innate qualities that are already who we are.

Another powerful form of loving-kindness is learning to do the practice, not as a guided meditation, but as individual play with the whole experience of quality of mind. Loving-kindness, or metta, done in this way bears some similarities to Thomas Keating's Centering Prayer and to John Main's and Laurence Freeman's Christian Meditation, though it is not identical with either one.

Loosely, the practice involves having the primary object of attention be the repeating of phrases, rather than attending to a word or the breath. As the practitioner repeats the phrases, s/he keeps in touch with the meaning of the words, and also with the object of the phrases (e.g., the self or others). When the attention wanders, it is kindly brought back to the phrases (as in training in mindfulness meditation, where the attention is kindly returned to the breath, the body and the breath, or an anchor point in the breath).

Practitioners are also invited to look for resonation or echo in the body, in the gestalt, or quality of mind. If such a quality becomes very intense or demanding, attention can rest in this experience. But if the mind wanders from the breath or any kinesthetic focus, attention is kindly returned, not to the breath or to resonation in the body (which may or may not be present), but to the phrases that were the initial object of attention. Then the process is begun again. Similar practices with varied phrases are repeated for work with other wholesome qualities of mind.

The resources for fostering wholesome qualities of mind are extensive. Some especially valuable and precise tools are offered in the Theravadan teachings. (See the recommended reading at the end of this chapter and in Appendix C, Recommended Reading by Category, Practice Manuals by Insight Meditation Teachers. These would be a good place to start. For further practices see under Christian Mystics, Vipassana, and Culture in Appendix C. I have included only a few of the many resources available in the Tibetan traditions.)

Practices for fostering heart qualities in any tradition, as opposed to opening to them through mindful attention, are interesting and powerful, but they can also be misused or overused like any other practice. We might be focusing too much on helping others, for instance, rather than taking the responsibility of paying attention to our own experience — and the one being we really can most readily impact. We can get so busy doing practices that we miss the primary intention: transformation or seeing clearly and accepting things as they are, including both what is ground consciousness and what is ordinary mind.

Self-questioning Strategies
(Challenging Our Assumptions or Views)

A tool we use in education to help students be aware of their cognitive processes and to evaluate cognitive effectiveness (metacognition) is self-questioning strategies. We can do this simply by turning strategies like those offered in this book into questions.[3] By asking questions, we engage mental participation without explicitly directing the process.

In this chapter, for example, previous headings were *Balancing* and *Fostering Wholesome Qualities of Mind*. Questions can be very general: *Am I fostering wholesome qualities of mind? In what areas of my life do I need to find balance? What wholesome qualities am I aware of experiencing?*

The questions can also be very specific, as in the exercise offered at the end of this chapter.

Questions can extend beyond the text, leading to further explorations: *What are some wholesome mind states? How do I recognize them? Do I lean more toward experience or away from it?*

The most important questions to ask are the ones we aren't supposed to ask, questions that challenge basic assumptions.[4] Asking such questions is pretty challenging to do by ourselves, because the beliefs are so basic, so interwoven in the experience of who we are.

Through mindfulness in our relationships, we can see ourselves reflected by others, a valuable support for this critical seeing. Another way to access our basic assumptions is to suspend belief in all our thoughts and challenge each one, especially those that cause pain and suffering. A quite safe test for assessing the authenticity of our thinking is to determine that it does not cause harm to others or ourselves.

Beginning Practice
for Shaping the Mind

Pay attention to whether or not the body feels balanced right now and periodically in the next few days.

Are your clothes comfortable, or are they too tight or too loose? It is amazing the discomfort we can tolerate without becoming aware of some simple, easy adjustments we could make.

Is your food intake about right, not too much and not too little? Are you feeling too full or empty? Is there discomfort from too much of a good thing, too many sweets, or something that just isn't right for your body chemistry?

Are you getting enough sleep? Enough exercise? Are you allowing adequate time for relationships?

Especially notice if your overall energy level is balanced. *Are you too intense, too busy, or too slow and sluggish?*

When in doubt, choose to be kind to yourself, as you would be kind but firm and protective with a precious child.

Open your heart to a difficult person. You don't need to contact him/her or do this in a state of anger toward that person. Just, alone in your room, open your heart. You can physically do so by letting your shoulders drop down and away from your ears and moving the shoulders back slightly to open the chest and heart area.

Ask yourself any time you remember, *Is this particular thought or perception really true?* It is not necessary to get too deeply absorbed in this activity. Simply asking the question and answering with deep honesty often reveals the lack of substantiality of the concern. We are usually creating fictions based on our past or on our fears of the future. This question is especially useful when we are creating our own suffering because of worry, guilt, anger, or shame.

If you catch yourself in an unskillful mind state like anger, jealousy, or some other form of grasping, even in an addictive type of behavior, choose to just stop. Turn to your breath, to your body, to physical sensations. You might even physically remove yourself from the circumstance. Be alone, if necessary, to fully explore and open to the quality of mind and its effects. What are the accompanying emotions? Notice body and breath, quality of breath, posture, places of tension and of openness, heart qualities, and any hollowness or emptiness. Let yourself stay with the direct experience without fanning flames through the content or stories about the experience.

Recommended Reading for Shaping the Mind

Boorstein, Sylvia. *Pay Attention, For Goodness' Sake: Practicing the Perfections of the Heart — the Buddhist Path of Kindness.*

Brown, Byron. *Soul Without Shame: A Guide to Liberating Yourself from the Judge Within.*

Gyatso, Geshe Kelsang. *Meaningful to Behold: The Bodhisattva's Way of Life.*

Hopkins, Jeffrey, et al., ed. and trans. *Compassion in Tibetan Buddhism.*

Kramer, Greg. *Meditating Together, Speaking from Silence: The Practice of Insight Dialogue.*

Macy, Joanna, and Molly Young Brown. *Coming Back to Life: Practices to Reconnect Our Lives, Our World.*

Salzberg, Sharon. *Lovingkindness: The Revolutionary Art of Happiness.*

Advanced Reading — Theravada Reference

Buddhaghosa, Bhadantacariya. *Visuddhimagga — The Path of Purification.*

CHAPTER FIVE — Conclusion

Birthing Embodied Being

When Moses descended the mountain
and came announcing a land flowing with milk and honey
that milk and honey was humanity and divinity.
Compassion flows when humanity and divinity flow.

—MEISTER ECKHART

Birthing is not easy, but it is possible. In fact, literal birthing is a normal occurrence. All species birth their own offspring, usually without teachers. We humans, however, need to make good use of our teachers so that all our efforts don't get in the way of whatever is unfolding. The body has intelligence of its own. The challenge is to participate without trying to stop it and without getting in the way.

A physical contraction in the birth process is just a contraction unless we name it pain. When we call it pain, we set up a struggle against it, instead of a willingness to simply allow what is. In allowing what is, though an experience may be exhausting, it may also be life-enhancing, bringing us deep satisfaction in having done well, having participated intelligently and fully with life. And often, like birthing our children, beautiful results spring forth.

The tools described in the preceding chapters help us open to our vulnerability and pain, as well as to what is beyond pain and suffering. They bring us in contact with what is real. If we can keep from taking preemptive action to remove or shield ourselves from experience (at least not without careful consideration), we may foster our spiritual maturation. We may allow ourselves to experience both our tenderness and our fear. We can then grow in our natural capacities for wholesome qualities of mind, such as loving-kindness and compassion.

We can usually open to these experiences by being intimate with our own immediate experience. Thought can drag us in deeper or separate us even further from our experience. So, instead of thinking our way through, we need to get beneath, or above, language and the conceptual mind. We need to experience life directly, being mindful in all circumstances, accepting it all just as it is, and not always wishing something to be different.

There is a desperate need throughout the planet for coming to truth about reality and our lack of connection to it, because of the harm we do to each other and ourselves when we are out of touch. We are sometimes even smug and righteous; sure that we are on the right side of any arguments or differences in opinions and beliefs, unwilling to hear the voices we disagree with. We have become numb, even intentionally self-medicating. We are out of touch not only with suffering throughout the world, but with our own suffering, our own vulnerability, our own capabilities of harming, our own human potential for descending into lost or desperate means.

Being out of touch with suffering means we are also out of touch with our real joy, with anything real. We lose connection with our great potential for participating in the creation of things that really matter.

A full and noble life requires being awake and mindful. It requires both willingness to surrender and an all-encompassing involvement in our own spiritual work and our own transformation. "Sanctity," according to Thomas Merton, a contemporary Christian mystic, "consists in perfect union of mind and will with God . . . perfect obedience. . . . The formula must not be oversimplified. It must not be applied mechanically and without understanding. It can never become a matter of routine, for the sanctity God asks of us is found not in obedience of mules but in the reasonable service proper to beings endowed with freedom and intelligence."[1]

We can use the body's knowing as a doorway to freedom, to real communion, to being human as sacrament. In surrendering in every moment, we come to the kingdom now. We train ordinary consciousness and identify with the heart/mind and the vast consciousness of which we are a part. The result is that instead of being battered by life, we stay in touch with powerful vital forces. In mindfulness, in openness and non-resistance to all life experience, we are free to create instead of merely defending or being trapped in a life of problem solving.

Our life can become prayer. We can experience it as we would the creation of music, with our whole bodies as instruments, like jazz musicians being able to stay in a groove. We may live in contentment with things as they are — aware of the blue sky, and, on occasion, cruise the updrafts, perhaps even be the updraft.

Initial Practices
for Birthing Embodied Being

Enjoy life! Say *Yes* to life!

Move — Develop skill or honor your interest in some activity that involves the whole body. Dance, ski, swim, canoe, or simply walk and move. The most normal state for a body is motion. Let it move and flow. Pay attention to it as it moves. What makes the activities a prayer practice, a way of embodiment, is doing them with full attention to the experience, to the flow of movement, to the subtle body sensations in all experiences, and also with awareness of the space within which all movement and physicality flow.

If you haven't been doing much movement, start with a massage or several weeks of massages. In fact, a massage is a good idea anytime. The best way to find a body worker you can be comfortable with is through the recommendation of someone you trust (friend, doctor, or therapist). Go to a professional and pay attention to the physical sensations in the body as s/he works. Don't let the massage be something someone is doing to you. Open to the skill of the body worker and let the whole body relax. Deep-seated wounds held in body memory can be healed without their ever having come to consciousness.

Create — Play with some artistic medium. It can be in the visual arts: in fabric art, needlework, painting, sculpting, drawing, creating in collage, print making, photography, computer art, graphic design; or in the performing arts: dancing, singing, playing music, acting. What is fun for you to do? Your life itself, the way you live, can be art, but it is fun to let creating unfold in a specific form as well.

Be faithful to your heart's deepest intentions. Revisit them every day and during the day. Let them expand and unfold.

Recommended Reading for Birthing Embodied Being

Amaro, Ajahn. *Small Boat, Great Mountain: Theravadan Reflections on the Natural Great Perfection.*

Aronson, Harvey. *Buddhist Practice on Western Ground: Reconciling Eastern Ideals and Western Psychology.*

Cameron, Julie, with Mark Bryan. *The Artist's Way: A Spiritual Path of Higher Creativity.*

Carse, James P. *Finite and Infinite Games.*

Epstein, Mark. *Going to Pieces Without Falling Apart: A Buddhist Perspective on Wholeness.*

———. *Open to Desire: Embracing a Lust for Life: Insights from Buddhism and Psychotherapy.*

Fritz, Robert. *Your Life as Art.*

Goldstein, Joseph. *One Dharma: The Emerging Western Buddhism.*

Klein, Anne C. *Meeting the Great Bliss Queen: Buddhists, Feminists, and the Art of the Self.*

Santorelli, Saki. *Heal Thyself: Lessons on Mindfulness in Medicine.*

Suzuki, Shunryu. *Zen Mind, Beginner's Mind.*

(See also under Vipassana and Culture in Appendix C, Recommended Reading by Category.)

This is my simple religion.
There is no need for temples;
No need for complicated philosophy.
Our own brain, our own heart is our temple;
The philosophy is kindness.

HIS HOLINESS
THE 14TH DALAI LAMA

EPILOGUE

The Kalamas's Dilemma
Adapted from the *Anguttara Nikaya*,
translated by Andrew Olendzki[1]

One time Buddha was walking on tour with a large group of monks, when he came to a town of the Kalamas called Kesaputta. The Kalamas of Kesaputta thought: "It is very good indeed to see Awakened Ones such as these." And so they went up to where Buddha was. Having seated themselves to one side, the Kalamas of Kesaputta said this to Buddha:

"There are, sir, many different teachers that come to Kesaputta. They illustrate and illuminate their own doctrines, but the doctrines of others they put down, revile, disparage, and cripple. For us, sir, uncertainty arises, and doubts arise concerning them: Who indeed of these venerable teachers speaks truly, who speaks falsely?"

"It is indeed fitting, Kalamas, to be uncertain, it is fitting to doubt. For in situations of uncertainty, doubts surely arise. You should decide, Kalamas, not by what you have heard, not by following convention, not by assuming it is so, not by relying on the texts, not because of reasoning, not because of logic, not by thinking about explanations, not by acquiescing to the views that you prefer, not because it appears likely, and certainly not out of respect for a teacher.

"When you would know, Kalamas, for *yourselves*, that 'These things are unhealthy, these things, when entered upon and undertaken, incline toward harm and suffering' — then, Kalamas, you should reject them.

"What do you think, Kalamas? When greed, hatred, or delusion arise within a person, does it arise for their welfare or their harm?"

"For their harm, sir."

"And when a person has become greedy, hateful, or deluded, their mind consumed by this greed, hatred, or delusion, Kalamas, do they kill living creatures, and take what has not been given, and go to another's spouse, and speak what is false, and induce others to undertake what is, for a long time, to their harm and suffering?"

"This is true, sir."

"And what do you think, Kalamas? Are these things healthy or unhealthy?"

"Unhealthy, sir."

"And when entered upon and undertaken, do they incline toward harm and suffering or don't they?"

"We agree, sir, that they do."

"But when you would know, Kalamas, for *yourselves*, that 'These things are healthy, these things, when entered upon and undertaken, incline toward welfare and happiness' — then, Kalamas, having come to them you should stay with them.

"What do you think, Kalamas? When nongreed, nonhatred, or nondelusion arise within a person, does it arise for their welfare or their harm?"

"For their welfare, sir."

"And when a person has not become greedy, hateful, or deluded, their mind not consumed by this greed, hatred, or delusion, Kalamas, do they not kill living creatures, and not take what has not been given, and not go to another's spouse, and not speak what is false, and induce others to undertake what is, for a long time, to their welfare and happiness?"

"This is true, sir."

"And what do you think, Kalamas? Are these things healthy or unhealthy?"

"Healthy, sir."

"And when entered upon and undertaken, do they incline toward welfare and happiness or don't they?"

"We agree, sir, that they do."

"That person, Kalamas, who is a follower of the noble path is thus free of wanting, free of harming, and without confusion. Clearly conscious and mindful, he or she abides having suffused the first direction, then the second, then the third and fourth — and so above, below and across, everywhere and in every way — with a mind dedicated to loving kindness, compassion, good will, and equanimity that is abundant, expansive, immeasurable, kindly, and free of harming.

"And so, Kalamas, the follower of the noble path whose mind is thus kindly and free of harming — their mind is not defiled, but is purified."

. . . I want to beg you, as much as I can, to be patient toward all that is unresolved in your heart and to try to love the questions themselves like locked rooms and like books that are written in a very foreign tongue. Do not now seek the answers, which cannot be given you because you would not be able to live them. And the point is, to live everything. Live the questions now. Perhaps you will then gradually, without noticing it, live along some distant day into the answer.

Resolve to be always beginning — to be a beginner! (Mood, 25)

I hold this to be the highest task of a bond between two people: that each should stand guard over the solitude of the other. For, if it lies in the nature of indifference and of the crowd to recognize no solitude, then love and friendship are there for the purpose of continually providing the opportunity for solitude. And only those are the true sharings which rhythmically interrupt periods of deep isolation. . . . (Mood, 27)

—RAINER MARIA RILKE
As quoted in John Mood's *Rilke on Love and Other Difficulties: Translations and Considerations of Rainer Maria Rilke*

APPENDICES

Appendix A
Prayers of Intention

Buddhist

Primary Buddhist prayers of intention include Taking Refuge, Taking Bodhisattva Vows, and Reciting the Four Noble Truths.

Taking Refuge

A most basic practice, taking refuge, is to take shelter in three fundamental supports, the Buddha, the Dhamma,[1] and the Sangha.

> I take refuge in the Buddha (*Buddha nature*).
> I take refuge in the Dhamma (*Truth or teachings*).
> I take refuge in the Sangha (*Community of teachers and peers*).

The taking of refuge has many layers of meaning, from simple and comforting to deep and profound. Catholic Christians cannot help but draw parallels with concepts of the Trinity. When I do so, I do it a little differently than I've seen done in other places:

Buddha or *Buddha nature*	Holy Spirit or affect, dynamism uniting the other two (maybe mediating space)
Dhamma or *Truth*	Father or Godhead, Ultimate Reality

Sangha or *Community*	Son, manifestation of love relationship in physical form

The refuge chant below is from Tibet. It incorporates the whole body and being and integrates it with vast space or clarity consciousness. I adapted it for personal use, adding body movements, from teachings of Tenzin Wangyal, at Rothko Chapel in Houston, Texas, January 2003.[2]

Sound	Focus of Attention	Visualization or Imagination
Ah	center of forehead	Opening to vast consciousness, clarity, and knowing
Om	throat (or heart)	Gathering in all the wholesome qualities from the clarity and vastness
Hung	heart (or belly)	Manifesting in daily life

Bodhisattva Vows

Taking the Bodhisattva vow is proclaiming intentions to stay active in the world until all beings are free and released from repeated cycles of suffering. It is understood, however, that in taking such a vow we are not going to achieve such a lofty goal through our own efforts, as product and action of ego; rather, we recognize that such attainment is only possible if Buddha nature is fully manifested in our being. Buddha nature is the necessary support or mode of being for accomplishing anything significant and can only occur if we do the work of realization.

Following are some popular ways of making the Bodhisattva vows.

I dedicate myself to my healing and liberation. May I practice for all beings who can't practice for themselves. May the benefits I receive from this practice and my intention to deepen touch all beings and all life everywhere.

—THICH NHAT HAHN

May the positive energies and fruits that manifest through this day's practice serve toward the welfare and awakening of all beings everywhere, which, of course, includes ourselves.

—MARCIA ROSE
Mountain Hermitage, 2005

May I quickly attain liberation
for the welfare, happiness, and awakening of all beings.
May the merit of my practice be joined with all the
     wholesome actions
of the three times (past, present, future) and together
     may it all be dedicated
to the welfare, the happiness, and the liberation of all beings.

—JOSEPH GOLDSTEIN
IMS winter retreat, 2002

Just as the earth and the other elements abundantly and perpetually
provide for the needs of beings in myriad ways,
may I, too, in as many ways as possible,
provide for the beings that fill space
until all of them have attained nirvana.

—SHANTIDEVA
From Kalu Rinpoche,
Luminous Mind: The Way of the Buddha

When we have attained the limits of space,
when sentient beings are all enlightened,
when karma and the afflictions have all been exhausted,
thus emptied, my vow will have come to an end.

—BHADRACARYAPRANINDHANA
From Kalu Rinpoche,
Luminous Mind: The Way of the Buddha

Generating the Mind for Enlightenment
Combined Refuge and Bodhisattva Vow

With a wish to free all beings
I shall always go for refuge
to the Buddha, Dharma, and Sangha,
until I reach full enlightenment.

Enthused by wisdom and compassion,
today in the Buddha's presence
I generate the Mind for Full Awakening
for the benefit of all sentient beings.

As long as space endures,
as long as sentient beings remain,
until then, may I, too, remain
and dispel the miseries of the world.

—Shantideva
Quoted by the Dalai Lama in *Lojong: Training the Mind*

Generation of Bodhichitta
Supporting Bodhisattva Vow

Aspiration

Just like those, who in the past have gone to bliss,
conceived the awakened attitude of mind
and in precepts of the Bodhisattvas
step by step abode and trained,

likewise, for the benefit of beings,
I will generate this attitude of mind,
and in those self-same precepts
step by step I will abide and train.

Application

May I be a guard for those who are protectorless,
a guide for those who journey on the road;
for those who wish to go across the water,
may I be a boat, a raft, a bridge.

May I be an isle for those who yearn for landfall,
and a lamp for those who long for the light;
for those who need a resting place, a bed;
for all who need a servant, may I be a slave.

May I be the wishing jewel, the vase of plenty,
a word of power, and the supreme remedy.
May I be the trees of miracles,
and for every being, the abundant cow.

Like the great earth and the other elements,
enduring as the sky itself endures,
for the boundless multitude of living beings,
may I be the ground and vessel of their life.

Thus, for every single thing that lives,
in number like the boundless reaches of the sky,
may I be their sustenance and nourishment
until they pass beyond the bounds of suffering.

—DALAI LAMA
A Flash of Lightning in the Dark of Night:
A Guide to the Bodhisattva's Way of Life

Four Noble Truths

The Four Noble Truths are the centerpiece of the Buddha's teaching and a unique offering of Buddhist thought, the Good News of Buddha's teaching. Unfortunately Buddhism has been incorrectly depicted as nihilistic, which is not the case at all. In fact, Buddhism does not address questions that cannot be answered through direct experience. By so doing, it leaves greater room for truth to speak for itself and prevents the appropriating of teaching to support any substantial (reified or idolized) humanly conceived image or objective.

Some renditions of the Four Noble Truths:

> There is suffering.
> Suffering has causes and conditions.
> Suffering can end.
> We end suffering following the eightfold path.

Or

> Phenomena that arise in conditioned reality are unsatisfactory
>   because, being conditioned, they cannot last.
> We suffer when we crave reality to be other than it is. This is the
>   suffering of clinging.
> Recognition of this unsatisfactoriness and letting go of clinging
>   are freeing.
> We follow the eightfold path to reach this understanding and to
>   live by it in happiness and ease of being.

Or

> Nothing is as substantial as it appears to be.
> Clinging to what is insubstantial causes suffering.
> Suffering ends with clarity and with the end of clinging.
> Living the eightfold path is both the way and a result.

Or more briefly:

> Phenomena arise.
> Our reaction or response
> conditions whatever follows.
> We can learn more skillful means.

Popular Christian Prayers

Lord, make me an instrument of your peace.
Where there is hatred, let me sow love,
where there is injury, pardon,
where there is doubt, faith,
where there is despair, hope,
where there is darkness, light,
and where there is sadness, joy.
O divine master, grant that I may
not so much seek to be consoled as to console,
to be understood as to understand,
to be loved as to love.
For it is in giving that we receive,
and it is in pardoning that we are pardoned,
and it's in dying that we are born to eternal life.

Amen.

—Prayer of ST. FRANCIS

My Lord God, I have no idea where I am going.

I do not see the road ahead of me. I cannot know for certain where it will end.

Nor do I really know myself, and the fact that I think I am following your will does not mean that I am actually doing so.

But I believe that the desire to please you does in fact please you and I hope that I have that desire in all that I am doing.

And I know that if I do this, you will lead me by the right road, although I may know nothing about it.

Therefore will I trust you always, though I may seem to be lost, and in the shadow of death, I will not fear, for you are ever with me and you will never leave me to face my perils alone.

—THOMAS MERTON
Prayer of Trust

O God, we pray for all those in our world who are suffering from
    injustice;
for those who are discriminated against because of their race, colour
    or religion;
for those imprisoned for working for the relief of oppression;
for those who are hounded for speaking the inconvenient truth:
for those tempted to violence as a cry against overwhelming hardship;
for those deprived of reasonable health and education;
for those suffering from hunger and famine;
for those too weak to help themselves and who have no one else to
    help them:
for the unemployed who cry out for work but do not find it.
We pray for anyone of our acquaintance who is personally affected
    by injustice.
Forgive us, Lord, if we unwittingly share in the conditions
    or in a system that perpetuates injustice.
Show us how we can serve your children and make your love practical
    by washing their feet.

—MOTHER TERESA

Deliver me, O Jesus,
from the desire to be loved,
from the desire to be extolled,
from the desire to be honored,
from the desire to be praised,
from the desire to be preferred,
from the desire to be consulted,
from the desire to be approved,
from the desire to be popular,

from the fear of being humiliated,
from the fear of being despised,
from the fear of being rebuked,
from the fear of being slandered,
from the fear of being forgotten,
from the fear of being wronged,
from the fear of being ridiculed,
from the fear of being suspected.

—MOTHER TERESA

~◌~◌~

Appendix B

Satipatthana Sutta
The Direct Path to Realization
(More commonly known as the Sutta on
the Four Foundations of Mindfulness)

The Satipatthana Sutta[3] encompasses most meditation teachings of the Pali Canon and can be approached, practiced, or taught from many different angles or in varied order. The Buddha reputedly said that if he spent his whole life teaching just this sutta, it would be time well spent.

Readers of Thomas Merton may be interested to know that this sutta was recommended in the writings of one of Merton's favorite authors, Aldous Huxley, at the time Merton entered monastic life. Huxley mentioned this sutta as a detailed exploration for coming to self-knowledge.

There is, for example, the Buddha, whose discourse on the "The Setting-Up of Mindfulness" expounds (with that positively inexorable exhaustiveness characteristic of the Pali scriptures) the whole art of self-knowledge in all its branches — knowledge of one's body, one's senses, one's feelings, one's thoughts.[4]

Huxley stressed primarily exploration of the four foundations, or the four satipatthanas, as objects of meditation. Though by themselves an invaluable gift, the sutta's teachings offer much more than this. One of its critical elements is dynamism, including interdependence, impermanence, flowing process, and the relationship between the satipatthanas.

I don't know if Thomas Merton ever worked with the sutta. During his lifetime he would most likely have been exposed to the teachings of this sutta through Theravada monks. Though the teachings are a foundational part of every Buddhist tradition, until recently the sutta has received little emphasis in the West except in the Theravada tradition, where it is the primary experiential teaching.

Work with these teachings can bring us to self-knowledge and to manifestation of our deepest understandings of wisdom in action. Though this sutta is most commonly known as the Sutta on the Four Foundations of Mindfulness or as the Four Frames of Reference, it has been most recently called The Direct Path to Realization.[5] This rendition stresses the importance of the four satipatthanas as words of action. Practitioners working with the teachings come to recognize not only constructions of the self and our various component parts, but also the interaction and mutually influencing nature of all phenomena and the relationship of all to the empty nature of phenomena. The sutta is about learning to manifest the teachings of the practice in our lives, to be the wisdom the sutta teaches.

There are two versions of this sutta in the Pali Canon: The Satipatthana Sutta in the *Middle Length Discourses*, and the Mahasatipattahana, or the Great Sutta on the Four Foundations of Mindfulness, in the *Long Discourses*. The longer version contains greater detail in the fourth satipatthana on dhammas or phenomena, particularly around the four noble truths.

Below are an outline and summary of the sutta, followed by a bibliography of writings about it. These writings include various translations. Online translations are also available on websites listed at the end of the bibliography.

Introduction

The sutta begins with the words, "Thus have I heard." This is a signal that the teachings are the words of the Buddha, recited by his student and assistant, Ananda, memorized by monks after the death of Gautama Buddha. The suttas were collected for oral recitation at the first Council about three months after the death of Gautama Buddha. At the time "recording" was done through memorization. Because the teachings, the suttas, were memorized and repeated over and over (chanted), sutta teachings are stated briefly and directly and with great redundancy. Yet they capture in brief and pithy phrases, in combination with wonderful stories, the central elements of the teachings. The suttas were handed down in this manner for five hundred years until they were put in written form on banana leaves in Sri Lanka.

The teachings are practices to explore. Through their use we can discover what is true.

The sutta describes four categories of experience, four satipatthanas, which together describe all aspects of human experience. The four satipatthanas include, from most basic to most inclusive:
(1) Experiences of the body and physical sensations
(2) Feeling tones, the automatic responses to stimuli of *pleasant, unpleasant, indifferent,* or *neutral*
(3) Qualities of mind or mind states, which include emotions and various kinds of consciousness
(4) Dhammas (dharmas or phenomena), basic teachings and their relationship with aspects, or sutta elements, as they unfold in experience.

Promises
At both the beginning and the end of the sutta, the Buddha promises not only that the path he is sharing will work, but that it is the most direct path to realization. Skillful attention to the four satipatthanas will result in:
• Purification
• Overcoming of sorrow and lamentation
• Ending of pain and grief
• Attainment of the right path (ability to live with skillful means)
• Realization of Nibbana (enlightenment)

The concluding segment of the sutta also includes promises that by practicing diligently for even a short period of time, one can attain realization either immediately or at the end of this lifetime.

Supportive Mental Qualities
Practitioners working with these teachings will develop skillful attention and a pliable mind, establishing the following mental qualities:
- Diligence
- Clear knowing
- Mindfulness
- Freedom from grasping and aversion

Primary Themes
Each segment of the sutta is followed by a refrain, like the chorus of a song, stressing a repeated description of how to practice:

- Observing the various objects of attention both in our own experience and in that of others, then seeing that the qualities are universal in nature, not just "mine" or "yours"

- Observing that all these phenomena arise and pass away (not just understanding this, but viscerally experiencing it as so)

- Observing and analyzing only to the point necessary for seeing and experiencing clearly

- Observing without clinging to or rejecting any experience

- Observing experience that comes from ordinary consciousness and from aspects of mind that operate outside our mechanistic understandings of mind and reality

The Four Satipatthanas

1. The Contemplation of the Body

Mindfulness of breathing — This segment sets up the foundational practice of concentration. The practitioner goes to a quiet place, sitting in an alert but comfortable posture and turning attention, bare attention with no overlay of thought, to just the body, particularly to the breath of the body, the breathing body, and, according to some commentaries, to spaciousness of mind and to the mutual nature of both space and mind/body.

The postures of the body — The practitioner applies bare attention and awareness not only to breathing and to body, but also to the body in all postures, specifically including sitting, standing, lying down, and walking.

Mindfulness with clear comprehension — The intention here is to move from simply being aware of experience through bare attention, a passive practice, to one of recognizing process, then choosing skillful actions and avoiding unskillful ones. The practice involves expanding mindful attention to all activities and movement.

The reflection on the parts of the body — In this practice attention is turned to the organs and fluids of the body. Attention to bodily parts is considered an especially good practice for those attached to beauty of the body, bringing the practitioner to familiarity with the ordinariness of its component parts. (It may also be helpful in reducing revulsion to parts of the body considered ugly or distasteful.)

The reflection on the material elements — Here, through exploration, the practitioner discovers that the body, like all other planetary life, is composed of four basic elements: earth or hardness and firmness, water or flow and movement, air or cohesion and lightness, and fire or temperature. (Space can also be included. Space is not mentioned specifically in the Satipatthana Sutta, but is present in other suttas.)

The nine cemetery contemplations — In this practice the practitioner becomes very clear about the temporary nature of being a body by visualizing or observing the decay of a corpse in its various stages of dissolution.

2. The Contemplation of Feeling

The contemplation of feeling most formally applies to amoebic-like responses to stimuli that arise below the level of conscious participation — instantaneous bodily reactions that trigger *pleasant, unpleasant, neutral,* or *indifferent* feeling tones. These feeling tones are not volitional. One can't cause them to happen or not happen, but can observe the way they influence the body and mind. In actual practice, the contemplation of feelings is more often involved a little further along in the process. Mindfulness or attention is turned toward subsequent experiences of grasping or aversion in response or reaction to the felt sense of *pleasant, unpleasant,* or *indifferent.* In daily life the process is often only noticed well into a reactive mind state or emotion.

3. The Contemplation of Consciousness or Mind States

Contemplation of consciousness refers to awareness of qualities or states of mind. Among the unwholesome are specifically mentioned the three poisons of anger or aversion, lust or grasping, and ignorance, plus a fourth, restlessness. Four wholesome states are also identified: liberated mind, concentrated mind, unsurpassable mind, and great mind.

4. The Contemplation of Mental Objects or Phenomena

This segment of the sutta introduces fundamental teachings. It invites exploration of these teachings and their relationship to aspects of experience previously investigated in the sutta.

The five hindrances — The basic qualities of mind that prevent clarity, mindfulness, and awareness are: restlessness, sloth and torpor, grasping, aversion, and doubt.

The five aggregates of clinging — Aggregates are elements of the process of consciousness or awareness. They include: body or materiality *(rūpa),* consciousness *(viññāna),* perception or cognitions *(saññā),* feeling *(vedanā),* and formations or volition *(saṅkhārā).*

The six internal and external sense bases — Sense bases include both the organs that receive information (eyes, ears, nose, tongue, skin and nervous system, and mind[6]), considered external sense bases, and the internal experiences of objects (seeing, hearing, smelling, tasting, touching or sensing, and thinking).

The seven factors of enlightenment (awakening factors) — The factors of enlightenment are wholesome factors of mind that both support mindfulness and arise because of it. They can be thought of as (1) mindfulness, the central and mediating factor; three calming factors: (2) tranquility, (3) concentration, and (4) equanimity; and three energizing or active factors: (5) investigation, (6) energy, and (7) joy.

The four noble truths — (1) There is suffering, (2) but there are causes for suffering (the fundamental cause is not seeing clearly, not seeing things as they are, and therefore clinging to them). (3) In recognizing causes, particularly lack of clarity, suffering can end. (4) The end of suffering can occur through clarity or through practice of the eightfold path. The eightfold path can most briefly be described in three categories: wisdom, concentration or mind training, and ethical behavior.

A way to describe the four noble truths phenomenologically is: (1) Phenomena arise. (2, 3) We react unconsciously or respond consciously. (4) Each response conditions succeeding arisings of phenomena and creates future circumstances dependent upon our current behavior. Skillful behavior conditions wholesome unfoldings. Unskillful behavior conditions unwholesome results. Wholesome responses create continued options for further freedom from suffering.

Bibliography of Translations, Commentaries, and Practice Manuals

Insight Meditation Teachers

Goldstein, Joseph. *The Experience of Insight: A Simple and Direct Guide to Buddhist Meditation.*

Goldstein, Joseph, and Jack Kornfield. *Seeking the Heart of Wisdom: The Path of Insight Meditation.*

Kornfield, Jack. *A Path with Heart: A Guide Through the Perils and Promises of Spiritual Life.*

Nisker, Wes. *Buddha Nature: Evolution as a Practical Guide to Enlightenment.*

Monastic Teachers

Analayo. *Satipatthana: The Direct Path to Realization.*

Hanh, Thich Nhat. *Transformation and Healing: The Sutra on the Four Establishments of Mindfulness.*

Nyanaponika Thera. *The Heart of Buddhist Meditation.*

Rahula, Walpola. *What the Buddha Taught.*

Silananda, U. *The Four Foundations of Mindfulness.*

Soma Thera. *The Way of Mindfulness: Satipatthana Sutta Commentary.*

Theravada Reference Texts

Buddhaghosa, Bhantacariya. *Visuddhimagga — The Path of Purification.*

Nanamoli, Bhikkhu, and Bhikkhu Bodhi, trans. *The Middle Length Discourses of Buddha: A New Translation of the* Majjhima Nikaya.

Walshe, Maurice, trans. *The Long Discourses of the Buddha: A Translation of the* Digha Nikaya.

Websites

www.accesstoinsight.org/canon/sutta/digha/dn22.html

www.accesstoinsight.org/canon/sutta/majjhima/mn010.html

www.accesstoinsight.org/lib/bps/wheels/wheel019.html

www.vipassana.com/meditation/foundations_of_mindfulness.html

Appendix C

Recommended Reading by Category

Buddhist Traditions and Other Eastern Resources

- Recommended First Readings in Buddhist Meditation 93
- Practice Manuals by Insight Meditation Teachers (Lay Teachers) 93
- Writings of Monastic Teachers in the Theravada Tradition 94
- Theravada Reference Books 95
- Websites — Vipassana, Insight Meditation, and Theravada Study Sites 96
- Other Buddhist Traditions — Selected Readings 96
- Emptiness and Dependent Arising (Two Views of Mind) 97
- Hindu 98
- Sufi or Islam 98

Christian Resources

- Contemporary Christian Mystics and Meditation Teachers — Selected Readings 98
- Classic Christian Mystics — A Beginning List 99
- Christian Philosophy / Theology — A Beginning List 101
- Websites — Early Christian Writings 101

Western Culture and Meditation

- Selected Readings in Psychology / Consciousness / Spirituality 102
- Recovery 104
- Art and Creativity 104

Buddhist Traditions and Other Eastern Resources

Recommended First Readings in Buddhist Meditation

Batchelor, Stephen. *The Awakening of the West: The Encounter of Buddhism and Western Culture.*

Byrom, Thomas, trans. *The Dhammapada: The Sayings of the Buddha.*

or

Cleary, Thomas, trans. *Dhammapada: The Sayings of the Buddha.*

Epstein, Mark. *Going to Pieces Without Falling Apart: A Buddhist Perspective on Wholeness; Lessons from Meditation and Psychotherapy.*

Goldstein, Joseph. *The Experience of Insight: A Simple and Direct Guide to Buddhist Meditation.*

————. *One Dharma: The Emerging Western Buddhism.*

Goldstein, Joseph, and Jack Kornfield. *Seeking the Heart of Wisdom: The Path of Insight Meditation.*

Gunaratana, Bhante Henepola. *Eight Mindful Steps to Happiness: Walking the Buddha's Path.*

Kornfield, Jack. *A Path with Heart: A Guide Through the Perils and Promises of Spiritual Life.*

Salzberg, Sharon. *Faith: Trusting Your Own Deepest Experience.*

Practice Manuals by Insight Meditation Teachers (Lay Teachers)

Boorstein, Sylvia. *Pay Attention, for Goodness' Sake: Practicing the Perfections of the Heart — the Buddhist Path of Kindness.*

Brach, Tara. *Radical Acceptance: Embracing Your Life with the Heart of a Buddha.*

Feldman, Christina. *Principles of Meditation*.

Fronsdal, Gil. *The Issue at Hand: Essays on Buddhist Mindfulness Practice*.

Harrison, Gavin. *In the Lap of the Buddha*.

Kornfield, Jack. *Teachings of the Buddha*, rev. ed.

Kramer, Greg. *Meditating Together, Speaking from Silence: The Practice of Insight Dialogue*.

Levine, Stephen. *A Gradual Awakening*.

————. A *Year to Live: How to Live This Year as If It Were Your Last*.

Macy, Joanna. *World as Lover, World as Self*.

Meadow, Mary Jo. *Gentling the Heart: Buddhist Loving-Kindness Practice for Christians*.

Nisker, Wes. *Buddha Nature: Evolution as a Practical Guide to Enlightenment*.

Rosenberg, Larry. *Breath by Breath: The Liberating Practice of Insight Meditation*.

Salzberg, Sharon. *Lovingkindness: The Revolutionary Art of Happiness*.

Smith, Rodney. *Lessons from the Dying*.

Titmuss, Christopher. *Light on Enlightenment: Revolutionary Teachings on the Inner Life*.

Weisman, Arinna, and Jean Smith. *The Beginner's Guide to Insight Meditation*.

Writings of Monastic Teachers in the Theravada Tradition

Amaro, Ajahn. *Small Boat, Great Mountain: Theravadan Reflections on the Natural Great Perfection*.

Buddhadasa, Bhikkhu. *Heartwood of the Bodhi Tree: The Buddha's Teaching on Voidness*.

Chah, Ajahn. *Being Dharma: Essence of the Buddha's Teaching.*

Khema, Ayya. *Who Is My Self? A Guide to Buddhist Meditation.*

Kornfield, Jack. *Living Dharma: Teachings of Twelve Buddhist Masters.*

Nyanaponika Thera. *The Heart of Buddhist Meditation.*

Rahula, Walpola. *What the Buddha Taught.*

Sumedho, Ajahn. *The Way It Is.*

Theravada Reference Books

Analayo. *Satipatthana: The Direct Path to Realization.*

Aronson, Harvey B. *Love and Sympathy in Theravada Buddhism.*

Bodhi, Bhikkhu. *The Connected Discourses of the Buddha: A New Translation of the* Samyutta Nikaya.

Buddhadasa, Bhikkhu. *Mindfulness with Breathing: A Manual for Serious Beginners.*

Buddhaghosa, Bhadantacariya. *Visuddhimagga — The Path of Purification.*

Flickstein, Matthew. *Swallowing the River Ganges: A Practical Guide to the Path of Purification.*

Mahasi Sayadaw. *The Progress of Insight: Through the Stages of Purification.*

Nanamoli, Bhikkhu (original translation) and Bhikkhu Bodhi, trans. *The Middle Length Discourses of the Buddha: A New Translation of the* Majjhima Nikaya.

Nyanaponika Thera. *Abhidhamma Studies: Researches in Buddhist Psychology.*

Pandita, Sayadaw U. *In This Very Life: The Liberation Teachings of the Buddha.*

Piyadassi Thera. *The Buddha's Ancient Path.*

Silananda, U. *The Four Foundations of Mindfulness.*

Soma Thera. *The Way of Mindfulness: Satipatthana Sutta Commentary.*

Walshe, Maurice, trans. *The Long Discourses of the Buddha: A Translation of the* Digha Nikaya.

Websites — Vipassana, Insight Meditation, and Theravada Study Sites

www.abhayagiri.org

www.accesstoinsight.org

www.amaravati.org

www.dharmastream.org

Other Buddhist Traditions — Selected Readings

Beck, Charlotte Joko. *Everyday Zen: Love and Work.*

Buswell, Robert E. *The Korean Approach to Zen: The Collected Works of Chinul.*

Buswell, Robert E., and Robert M. Gimello. *Paths to Liberation: The Marga and Its Transformations in Buddhist Thought.*

Chodron, Pema. *The Places That Scare You: A Guide to Fearlessness in Difficult Times.*

Dalai Lama. *The Dalai Lama at Harvard.*

———. *Transforming the Mind: Teachings on Generating Compassion.*

Hanh, Thich Nhat. *Transformation and Healing: The Sutra on the Four Establishments of Mindfulness.*

Klein, Anne C. *Meeting the Great Bliss Queen: Buddhists, Feminists, and the Art of the Self.*

Norbu, Chogyal Namkhai. *Dzogchen: The Self-Perfected State.*

Shantideva, Acharya. *Bodhisattvacharyavatara — A Guide to the Bodhisattva's Way of Life*.

Suzuki, Shunryu. *Zen Mind, Beginner's Mind*.

Trungpa, Chogyam. *Cutting Through Spiritual Materialism*.

Williams, Angel Kyodo. *Being Black: Zen and the Art of Living with Fearlessness and Grace*.

Emptiness and Dependent Arising (Two Views of Mind)

Amaro, Ajahn. *Small Boat, Great Mountain: Theravadan Reflections on the Natural Great Perfection*.

Buddhadasa, Bhikkhu. *Heartwood of the Bodhi Tree: The Buddha's Teaching on Voidness*.

Hopkins, Jeffrey. *Meditation on Emptiness*.

Klein, Anne C. *Path to the Middle*.

Macy, Joanna. *Mutual Causality in Buddhism and General Systems Theory: The Dharma of Natural Systems*.

———. *World as Lover, World as Self*.

Nagao, Gadjin. *The Foundational Standpoint of Madhyamika Philosophy*.

Napper, Elizabeth. *Dependent Arising and Emptiness*.

Newland, Guy. *The Two Truths*.

Rabten, Geshe. *Echoes of Voidness*.

Talbot, Michael. *The Holographic Universe*.

Von Bruck, Michael. "Buddhist Sunyata and the Christian Trinity: The Emerging Holistic Paradigm" in *Buddhist Emptiness and Christian Trinity*, ed. Roger Corless and Paul F. Knitter.

Hindu

Krishna, Gopi. *Kundalini: The Evolutionary Energy of Man.*

Nisargadatta Maharaj. *I Am That: Talks with Sri Nisargadatta.*

Sufi or Islam

Feild, Reshad. *Steps to Freedom.*

Hafiz. *The Gift: Poems by Hafiz, The Great Sufi Master*, trans. David Ladinsky.

Kabir. *The Kabir Book: Forty-Four of the Ecstatic Poems of Kabir*, trans. Robert Bly.

Rumi. *Open Secret: Versions of Rumi*, trans. John Moyne and Coleman Barks.

Shah, Idries. *Learning How to Learn: Psychology and Spirituality in the Sufi Way.*

Tweedie, Irina. *The Chasm of Fire: A Woman's Experience with the Teachings of a Sufi Master.*

Christian Resources

Contemporary Christian Mystics and Meditation Teachers — Selected Readings

Cardenal, Ernesto. *To Live Is to Love.*

Culligan, Kevin, Mary Jo Meadow, and Daniel Chowning. *Purifying the Heart: Buddhist Insight Meditation for Christians.*

De Mello, Anthony, SJ. *Awareness: The Perils and Opportunities of Reality; A De Mello Spirituality Conference in His Own Words.*

———. *Sadhana: A Way to God.*

Finley, James. *Merton's Palace of Nowhere: A Search for God through Awareness of the True Self.*

Freeman, Laurence. *Jesus the Teacher Within.*

Hays, Edward. *Pray All Ways.*

Keating, Thomas. *Open Mind, Open Heart: The Contemplative Dimension of the Gospel.*

Merton, Thomas. *New Seeds of Contemplation.*

———. *Thoughts in Solitude: Meditations on the Spiritual Life and Man's Solitude before God.*

Nemeck, Francis Kelly, OMI, and Marie Theresa Coombs, Hermit. *O Blessed Night: Recovering from Addiction, Codependence, and Attachment Based on the Insights of St. John of the Cross and Pierre Teilhard de Chardin.*

Nouwen, Henri J. M. *The Way of the Heart.*

———. *With Open Hands.*

———. *The Wounded Healer.*

Roberts, Bernadette. *The Experience of No-Self: A Contemplative Journey.*

Rohr, Richard. *Everything Belongs: The Gift of Contemplative Prayer.*

Teilhard de Chardin, Pierre. *The Divine Milieu.*

———. *The Phenomenon of Man.*

Vanier, Jean. *From Brokenness to Community.*

Classic Christian Mystics — A Beginning List

Chittister, Joan, OSB. *The Rule of Benedict: Insights for the Ages.*

———. *Wisdom Distilled from the Daily: Living the Rule of St. Benedict Today.*

Clarke, John, OCD, trans. *Story of a Soul: The Autobiography of Saint Thérèse of Lisieux*.

Colledge, Edmond, OSA, and James Walsh, SJ, trans. and introduction. *Julian of Norwich: Showings*.

De Caussade, Jean Pierre. *Abandonment to Divine Providence*.

———. *The Sacrament of the Present Moment*.

Fox, Matthew. *Breakthrough: Meister Eckhart's Creation Spirituality in New Translation*.

Henry, Patrick, ed. *Benedict's Dharma: Buddhists Reflect on the Rule of St. Benedict*.

Kavanaugh, Kieran, OCD, and Otilio Rodriguez, OCD, trans. *The Collected Works of St. John of the Cross*.

Lawrence, Brother. *The Practice of the Presence of God: With Spiritual Maxims*.

Levko, John J. *Cassian's Prayer for the 21st Century*.

Palmer, G. E. H., Philip Sherrard, and Kallistos Ware, ed. and trans. *The Philokalia: The Complete Text of St. Nikodimos of the Holy Mountain and St. Makarios of Corinth*.

Peers, E. Allison, trans. *Interior Castles — Saint Theresa of Avila*.

Plattig, Michael, O. Carm. "Freedom to Souls: Spiritual Accompaniment According to the Carmelite Tradition," in *Tending the Holy: Spiritual Direction Across Traditions*, ed. Norvene Vest.

Radier, Beatrice, ed. *The Cloud of Unknowing and Other Works*.

Toner, Jules J. *A Commentary on St. Ignatius' Rules for the Discernment of Spirits*.

Ward, Benedicta, SLG, trans. *The Sayings of the Desert Fathers*.

Christian Philosophy/Theology — A Beginning List

Fox, Matthew. *Original Blessing: A Primer in Creation Spirituality.*

Funk, Robert W., Roy W. Hoover, and the Jesus Seminar. *The Five Gospels: What Did Jesus Really Say? The Search for the Authentic Words of Jesus.*

Groeschel, Benedict J. *Spiritual Passages: The Psychology of Spiritual Development.*

Hick, John, and Paul F. Knitter, eds. *The Myth of Christian Uniqueness: Toward a Pluralistic Theology of Religions.*

Keenan, John P. *The Gospel of Mark: A Mahayana Reading.*

McBrien, Richard P. *Catholicism.*

Peck, M. Scott. *People of the Lie: The Hope for Healing Human Evil.*

Swidler, Leonard, ed. *Toward a Universal Theology of Religion.*

Teilhard de Chardin, Pierre. *The Divine Milieu.*

———. *The Phenomenon of Man.*

Thompson, Helen, BVM. *Journey Toward Wholeness: A Jungian Model of Adult Spiritual Growth.*

Walsh, John. *Evangelization and Justice: New Insights for Christian Ministry.*

Websites — Early Christian Writings

www.ccel.org (Christian Classic Ethereal Library)

www.fordham.edu/halsall/sbook.html (Internet Medieval Sourcebook)

www.earlychristianwritings.com/ (Early Christian Writings)

Western Culture and Meditation

Selected Readings in Psychology / Consciousness / Spirituality

Abram, David. *The Spell of the Sensuous: Perception and Language in a More-Than-Human World.*

Almaas, A. H. *Diamond Heart Series* and *Diamond Mind Series.*

———. *The Pearl Beyond Price — Integration of Personality into Being: An Object Relations Approach.*

Aronson, Harvey B. *Buddhist Practice on Western Ground: Reconciling Eastern Ideals and Western Psychology.*

Bennett-Goleman, Tara. *Emotional Alchemy: How the Mind Can Heal the Heart.*

Brach, Tara. *Radical Acceptance: Embracing Your Life with the Heart of a Buddha.*

DeCharms, Christopher. *Two Views of Mind: Abhidharma and Brain Science.*

Epstein, Mark. *Going to Pieces Without Falling Apart: A Buddhist Perspective on Wholeness; Lessons from Meditation and Psychotherapy.*

———. *Open to Desire: Embracing a Lust for Life: Insights from Buddhism and Psychotherapy.*

———. "The Psychodynamics of Meditation: Pitfalls on the Spiritual Path." *Journal of Transpersonal Psychology.*

———. *Thoughts Without a Thinker: Psychotherapy from a Buddhist Perspective.*

Gendlin, Eugene T. *Focusing*, rev. ed.

Goleman, Daniel. *Destructive Emotions: How Can We Overcome Them? A Scientific Dialogue with the Dalai Lama.*

Hooks, Bell. *All About Love: New Visions.*

Katie, Byron. *Loving What Is: Four Questions That Can Change Your Life.*

Nelson, John E. *Healing the Split: Integrating Spirit Into Our Understanding of the Mentally Ill.*

Ouspensky, P. D. *The Psychology of Man's Possible Evolution.*

Podvoll, Edward M. *Recovering Sanity: A Compassionate Approach to Understanding and Treating Psychosis.*

Santorelli, Saki. *Heal Thyself: Lessons on Mindfulness in Medicine.*

Segal, Zindel V., J. Mark G. Williams, and John D. Teasdale. *Mindfulness-Based Cognitive Therapy for Depression: A New Approach to Preventing Relapse.*

Tolle, Eckhart. *The Power of Now: A Guide to Spiritual Enlightenment.*

Walsh, Roger. *Staying Alive: The Psychology of Human Survival.*

Walsh, Roger, and Frances Vaughan. "The Art of Transcendence: An Introduction to Common Elements of Transpersonal Practices." *The Journal of Transpersonal Psychology.*

Watts, Alan. *The Wisdom of Insecurity.*

Welwood, John, ed. *Awakening the Heart: East/West Approaches to Psychotherapy and the Healing Relationship.*

———. *Journey of the Heart: The Path of Conscious Love.*

Wilber, Ken, Jack Engler, and Daniel P. Brown. *Transformations of Consciousness: Conventional and Contemplative Perspectives on Development.*

Zajonc, Arthur, ed. *The New Physics and Cosmology: Dialogues with the Dalai Lama.*

Recovery

Ash, Mel. *The Zen of Recovery.*

Dodes, Lance. *The Heart of Addiction.*

May, Gerald G. *Addiction and Grace: Love and Spirituality in the Healing of Addictions.*

———. *The Awakened Heart: Living Beyond Addiction.*

Nemeck, Francis Kelly, OMI, and Marie Theresa Coombs, Hermit. *O Blessed Night: Recovering from Addiction, Codependence, and Attachment Based on the Insights of St. John of the Cross and Pierre Teilhard de Chardin.*

Art and Creativity

Arnheim, Rudolf. *Visual Thinking.*

Bayles, David, and Ted Orland. *Art and Fear: Observations on the Perils (and Rewards) of Artmaking.*

Cameron, Julie, with Mark Bryan. *The Artist's Way: A Spiritual Path of Higher Creativity.*

Franck, Frederick. *Zen Seeing, Zen Drawing: Meditation in Action.*

Fritz, Robert. *The Path of Least Resistance: Learning to Become the Creative Force in Your Own Life.*

———. *Your Life as Art.*

ENDNOTES

Introduction

1. Not all Christians accept this view of Jesus as both fully human and fully divine, nor do they see human beings as capable of achieving the same. In some Christian schools human beings are considered innately bad or sinful. Rather than seeing the crucifixion and resurrection as a model to follow, as a powerful image of the integrity and wisdom in nonviolence and surrender of self, they see the crucifixion as punishment that Jesus took on our behalf to compensate for human darkness. However, we can instead recognize ourselves not as dark, but as blind or ignorant to the harm that we do, blind to the innate beauty and wholeness of our true nature, and blind to what is really loving and true.

2. 2 Cor 3:18 "And all of us, with our unveiled faces like mirrors reflecting the glory of the Lord, are being transformed into the image that we reflect in brighter and brighter glory . . ." And from Meister Eckhart, as quoted by Matthew Fox in *Coming of the Cosmic Christ*: "Though we are God's sons and daughters, we do not realize it yet."

3. Sacraments in Catholic Christian teachings are celebrations of Divinity manifesting in humanity. Our role as co-creators with the Great Mystery is intentional participation in the divinizing of all existence. Sacraments call us to being human at its fullest, "made in the image and likeness of God" — a powerful teaching if not confused with its near enemy: God as image and likeness of us. This twist takes the teaching into a heresy through idolatry or false images of a "God" made to our own liking. Protection from this heresy lies in the Buddhist practice of following the Middle Way. We don't take any philosophizing too seriously, but focus on skillful means in the current moment and in evermore moments. Being in touch with what is true in our immediate experience, we choose to

be kind and not cause harm.

4. "Yes, Kalamas, it is proper that you have doubt, that you have perplexity, for a doubt has arisen in a matter which is doubtful. Now, look you Kalamas, do not be led by reports, or tradition, or hearsay. Be not led by the authority of religious texts, nor by mere logic or inference, nor by considering appearances, nor by the delight in speculative opinions, nor by seeming possibilities, nor by the idea: 'this is our teacher'. But, O Kalamas, when you know for yourselves that certain things are unwholesome (*akusala*), and wrong, and bad, then give them up . . . And when you know for yourselves that certain things are wholesome (*kusala*) and good, then accept them and follow them." (Rahula, quoting from an early translation of the *Digha Nikaya*, in *What the Buddha Taught*, 2–3.)

5. For powerfully and elegantly explicated support for the knowing available to us outside language and concepts, see Abram, *The Spell of the Sensuous: Perception and Language in a More-Than-Human World*.

CHAPTER ONE **Coming Home Through Our Senses**

1. See Culligan and Jordan, *Carmel and Contemplation: Transforming Human Consciousness*; Wilber, Engler, and Brown, *Transformations of Consciousness: Conventional and Contemplative Perspectives on Development*; Dalai Lama, *Transforming the Mind: Teachings on Generating Compassion*.

2. Heart/mind, *citta* in Pali ('c' pronounced as *ch*), *chitta* in Sanskrit. The English word *mind* is too limited for our purposes here. Citta embraces mind, heart, and consciousness. Ajahn Amaro points to the mind as radiant in this comment: "There is a beautiful expression that the Buddha used, the *pabhassara citta* — the radiant mind, the mind of clear light. He pointed out very clearly that the mind's nature is inherently radiant. Its brightness is not something that we have to produce; rather it is the intrinsic nature of mind, the citta." Amaro, *Silent Rain*, 92.

3. See Appendix C, Recommended Reading by Category: Emptiness and Dependent Arising, for writings on the Two Views of Mind.

4. A word from Tibetan Dzogchen teachings that means the innermost nature of mind.

5. The connections of mediating space with illumination and liminal space are the result of experiences at the 2004 Conference of Spiritual Direction International in Miami, Florida, where I first presented this material. Richard Rohr, OFM (Center for Action and Contemplation in Albuquerque, New Mexico), the keynote speaker, spoke powerfully of liminal space and its great importance in spiritual practice. Dr. Michael Plattig, O. Carm. (Spiritual Director for Carmelites of the Upper, southern, Province of Germany and recognized authority on the teachings of John of the Cross), spoke about stages of Christian development and relationship to Spiritual Direction. I heard from Michael Plattig, in particular, some important distinctions between Christian spiritual stages of illumination and unification. Illuminative states are more common than we think. Unification is also more accessible than we think, but, like full enlightenment, is rare and usually momentary.

6. For a starting point to understand what appears at first to be a magical idea, see Talbot's *Holographic Universe*. For a developing explanation via the interface between Buddhist teaching and Western science, see Zajonc, *The New Physics and Cosmology: Dialogues with the Dalai Lama*.

7. See research emanating from the Mind and Life Institute conferences at www.mindandlife.org. Among the books coming out of these conferences is Goleman's *Destructive Emotions: How Can We Overcome Them? A Scientific Dialogue with the Dalai Lama*. Also see research done at or through the Center for Mindfulness in Medicine, Health Care, and Society at www.umassmed.edu/cfm and the early work by Kabat-Zinn, *Full Catastrophe Living: Using the Wisdom of Your Body and Mind to Face Stress, Pain, and Illness*.

8. "As recently as the late 1980s the human brain was considered
to be a sort of biological computer that, as one scientist put it,
'secretes thoughts the way kidneys secrete urine.' We now know
that the brain is much more malleable and fluidly organized than
the analogy to computer hardware suggests, and that it changes
with every perception and every action." (James Shreeve, "Beyond
the Brain," *National Geographic*, March 2005, 26.) "One of the
main arguments for developing the analogy of the brain as a stable
machine or computer was that it helped to explain how we can
remember things from one instance to the next. . . . However,
we have learned that the brain is not physically stable, and that
is probably a good thing. The structural instability that we have
documented in the brain may be required to provide the extra
capacity that is necessary for dealing with complexity and to
provide the underpinning for the adaptability and flexibility, or
'plasticity' (as neuroscientists refer to it), that is required for dealing
with the variety of ever-changing challenges that we are faced with
throughout our entire lives." (Fred H. Gage," Structural Changes in
the Adult Brain in Response to Experience," presentation, October
18, 2004, at the Mind & Life Institute conference in Dharamsala,
India: Neuroplasticity: The Neuronal Substrates of Learning and
Transformation.)

9. For the most recent information, see research from the Mind
and Life Institute at www.mindandlife.org. The site provides
information about research and events emanating from regularly
scheduled explorations between scientists and the Dalai Lama.
See particularly Sharon Begley, "Scans of Monks' Brains Show
Meditation Alters Structure, Functioning," *Wall Street Journal*,
November 5, 2004. "Neuroplasticity . . . The term refers to the
brain's recently discovered ability to change its structure and function,
in particular by expanding or strengthening circuits that are used
and by shrinking or weakening those that are rarely engaged."

10. Ibid. Quoting Professor Richard Davidson, " . . . suggesting that mental training can bring the brain to a greater level of consciousness . . . [During meditative practice of compassion] activity in the left prefrontal cortex (the seat of positive emotions such as happiness) swamped activity in the right prefrontal (site of negative emotions and anxiety), something never before seen from purely mental activity."

11. Ibid. " . . . opens up the tantalizing possibility that the brain, like the rest of the body, can be altered intentionally. Just as aerobics sculpt the muscles, so mental training sculpts the gray matter in ways scientists are only beginning to fathom."

12. Though transformed in personal use, this clustering of *knowing*, *freeing*, and *shaping* originated in Nyanaponika's discussion of the threefold value of bare attention in *The Heart of Buddhist Meditation*, 34-45.

CHAPTER TWO **Knowing the Mind**

1. Sacks, "To See and Not See," in *An Anthropologist on Mars*, 108–152.

2. Physical insubstantiality is not addressed in all Buddhist schools. A more common understanding of insubstantiality, included in all traditions, is insubstantiality in relationship to concepts or views about life. However, modern-day physics and cognitive sciences are tantalizing wider acceptance of the more physically inclusive schools of thought. "With the opening of the twentieth century, the theories of quantum mechanics and relativity would make incomparable demands on our conception of the universe. We are still struggling to grasp their full implications . . . both quantum theory and relativity grant a new prominence to the observer. It is hard to overestimate the significance of these developments . . . changing our very notions of space and time, the ultimate nature of matter, and the evolution of the universe." (Zajonc, *The New Physics and Cosmology: Dialogues with the Dalai Lama*, 5.)

3. Khema, *When the Iron Eagle Flies: Buddhism for the West*, 15.

4. Ibid.

5. The sources of the basic meditation practices offered in this segment include a sutta (teaching of the Buddha from the earliest Buddhist canon, the Pali texts of Theravada Buddhism), particularly as offered in Burmese and Thai Forest traditions: The Satipatthana Sutta. See Appendix B for a summary of the sutta, a bibliography of translations and commentaries, and web links to writings and monastic sites. The Insight Meditation Network is the primary purveyor of these teachings in Western cultures. See websites of the primary centers (Insight Meditation Society (IMS) in Barre, Mass., at www.dharma.org; Spirit Rock near San Francisco, Calif., at www.spiritrock.org; and Gaia House in Devon, England, at www.gaiahouse.org), as well as many smaller local sites, including the author's site (www.citta101.org).

6. *Implicate* ("enfolded") is a word used by David Bohm to express a concept previously unconceived in Western thought — a pervasive context of everything (which includes chaos and order, all objects and events, visible or invisible) that either may have arisen into our field of perception or is not now apparent. Michael Talbot makes Bohm much easier to understand. Here are Talbot's comments introducing implicate and explicate order: "One of Bohm's most startling assertions is that the tangible reality of our everyday lives is really a kind of illusion, like a holographic image. Underlying it is a deeper order of existence, a vast and more primary level of reality that gives birth to all the objects and appearances of our physical world in much the same way that a piece of holographic film gives birth to a hologram. Bohm calls this deeper level of reality the *implicate* (which means "enfolded") order, and he refers to our own level of existence as the *explicate*, or unfolded, order." (Talbot, *Holographic Universe*, 46.)

7. Talbot, *Holographic Universe*. For in-depth explication, see Bohm, *Wholeness and the Implicate Order*. For a discussion of the knowledge and debate about these ideas, see Zajonc, *The New Physics and Cosmology*.

8. To help open the mind to this understanding, see Talbot, *Holographic Universe*, and Macy, *Mutual Causality in Buddhism and General Systems Theory*.

9. Piburn, *The Dalai Lama: A Policy of Kindness*, 77.

10. Guy Armstrong, teaching in a six-week retreat at IMS, winter 2002, translated this understanding into practices of concentration and insight — connecting clarity with concentration practices (*samadhi*) and knowing with insight (*vipassana*).

11. As defined by Analayo in *Satipatthana: The Direct Path to Realization*, 136, footnote 78.

12. Bodhi, *The Connected Discourses of the Buddha: A New Translation of the* Samyutta Nikaya; and *Transcendental Dependent Arising: A Translation and Exposition of the Upanisa Sutta*. www.accesstoinsight.org

13. According to Houston massage therapist and massage teacher Bruce Jones, RMT, MTI, approximately 90 percent of pain is soft tissue pain and is therefore responsive to non-invasive treatments. He was, of course, referring to the benefits of skilled bodywork, but this amenability to natural therapies supports the feasibility of healing through other alternative means, including mindful attention.

CHAPTER THREE Freeing the Mind

1. In Buddhist understanding, we actually might think of this in reverse: as fear creating the ego. Ego or contractions arise when fear arises or resistance is present.

2. See the creating process taught by Fritz in *Your Life as Art*. My discussion of creating as part of an exploration of learning to create

from what might be considered a non-dual orientation does not represent his work or teaching, though I am inspired by his work and influenced by it. I see many parallels in his work and the teachings I am sharing. I also get practical advice in his teaching for moving from the cushion to action.

3. This practice is thanks to Ajahn Amaro, *Small Boat, Great Mountain*, 30–31.

CHAPTER FOUR **Shaping the Mind**

1. Gendlin, *Focusing*, rev. ed., 32–36.

2. Tolle, *The Power of Now: A Guide to Spiritual Enlightenment*, 29–35.

3. For a list of such questions, see Rees, *Transforming the Power of Anger and Resentment: Self-Questioning Strategies*.

4. Bohm, *Thought as a System*; Katie, *Loving What Is: Four Questions That Can Change Your Life*.

CHAPTER FIVE **Birthing Embodied Being**

1. Merton, *The Ascent to Truth*, 187.

EPILOGUE

1. First published in Kornfield, *Teachings of the Buddha*, rev. ed., 93–95. Used by permission of the translator, Andrew Olendzki, Executive Director of the Barre Center for Buddhist Studies in Barre, MA.

APPENDICES

1. *Dhamma* is a Pali word. The more common spelling in the West is *Dharma*, a Sanskrit word. Pali is the language of the teachings in

Theravada traditions, which are the earliest writings, those recorded closest to the Buddha's death.

2. For Wangyal's original chant, see his *Healing with Form, Energy and Light: The Five Elements in Tibetan Shamanism, Tantra, and Dzogchen.*

3. *Sutta* is the Pali word for the recorded teachings of the Buddha; more common is the Sanskrit *Sutra.*

4. Huxley, *The Perennial Philosophy*, 162.

5. Analayo, *Satipatthana: The Direct Path to Realization.*

6. In Buddhist psychology the mind is considered one of the sense doors. There are six senses, not just five.

Alphabetical Bibliography

Abram, David. *The Spell of the Sensuous: Perception and Language in a More-Than-Human World.* New York: Vintage Books / Random House, 1997.

Almaas, A. H. *Diamond Heart Series* and *Diamond Mind Series.* Berkeley, CA: Diamond Books, 1987.

———. *The Pearl Beyond Price — Integration of Personality into Being: An Object Relations Approach.* Vol. 2 of *Diamond Mind Series.* Berkeley, CA: Diamond Books, 1988.

Amaro, Ajahn. *Silent Rain.* Redwood Valley, CA: Abhayagiri Forest Monastery, 1996.

———. *Small Boat, Great Mountain: Theravadan Reflections on the Natural Great Perfection.* Redwood Valley, CA: Abhayagiri Monastery, 2003.

Analayo. *Satipatthana: The Direct Path to Realization.* Birmingham, UK: Windhorse Publications, 2003.

Arnheim, Rudolf. *Visual Thinking.* Berkeley: University of California Press, 1969.

Aronson, Harvey B. *Buddhist Practice on Western Ground: Reconciling Eastern Ideals and Western Psychology.* Boston: Shambhala Publications, 2004.

———. *Love and Sympathy in Theravada Buddhism.* Delhi: Motilal Banarsidass, 1980.

Ash, Mel. *The Zen of Recovery.* New York: Putnam, 1993.

Batchelor, Stephen. *The Awakening of the West: The Encounter of Buddhism and Western Culture.* Berkeley, CA: Parallax Press, 1994.

Bayles, David, and Ted Orland. *Art and Fear: Observations on the Perils (and Rewards) of Artmaking.* Santa Barbara, CA: Capra Press, 1993.

Beck, Charlotte Joko. *Everyday Zen: Love and Work.* San Francisco: Perennial Library / Harper & Row, 1989.

Bennett-Goleman, Tara. *Emotional Alchemy: How the Mind Can Heal the Heart.* New York: Three Rivers Press, 2001.

Bodhi, Bhikkhu. *The Connected Discourses of the Buddha: A New Translation of the* Samyutta Nikaya. 2 vols. Boston: Wisdom Publications, 2000.

——. *Transcendental Dependent Arising: A Translation and Exposition of the Upanisa Sutta.* The Wheel Publication No. 277/278. Kandy, Sri Lanka: Buddhist Publication Society, 1980.

Bohm, David. *Thought as a System.* New York: Routledge, 1992.

——. *Wholeness and the Implicate Order.* New York: Routledge Classics, 2002. First published 1980 by Routledge.

Boorstein, Sylvia. *Pay Attention, For Goodness' Sake: Practicing the Perfections of the Heart — the Buddhist Path of Kindness.* New York: Ballantine Books, 2002.

Brach, Tara. *Radical Acceptance: Embracing Your Life with the Heart of a Buddha.* New York: Bantam Books, 2003.

Brown, Byron. *Soul Without Shame: A Guide to Liberating Yourself from the Judge Within.* Boston: Shambhala Publications, 1999.

Buddhadasa, Bhikkhu. *Heartwood of the Bodhi Tree: The Buddha's Teaching on Voidness.* Boston: Wisdom Publications, 1994.

——. *Mindfulness with Breathing: A Manual for Serious Beginners.* Translated by Satikaro Bhikkhu. Boston: Wisdom Publications, 1998.

Buddhaghosa, Bhadantacariya. *Visuddhimagga — The Path of Purification.* Translated by Bhikkhu Nanamoli. Kandy, Sri Lanka: Buddhist Publication Society, 1991.

Buswell, Robert E. *The Korean Approach to Zen: The Collected Works of Chinul.* Honolulu: University of Hawaii Press, 1983.

Buswell, Robert E., and Robert M. Gimello. *Paths to Liberation: The Marga and Its Transformations in Buddhist Thought.* Honolulu: University of Hawaii Press, 1992.

Byrom, Thomas, trans. *The Dhammapada: The Sayings of the Buddha.* Boston: Shambhala Publications, 1993.

Cameron, Julie, with Mark Bryan. *The Artist's Way: A Spiritual Path of Higher Creativity.* New York: Putnam, 1992.

Cardenal, Ernesto. *Abide in Love.* Maryknoll, NY: Orbis Books, 1995.

———. *To Live Is to Love.* New York: Herder & Herder, 1972.

Carse, James P. *Finite and Infinite Games.* Reissue ed. New York: Ballantine Books, 1987.

Chah, Ajahn. *Being Dharma: Essence of the Buddha's Teaching.* Translated by Paul Breiter. Boston: Shambhala Publications, 2001.

Chittister, Joan, OSB. *The Rule of Benedict: Insights for the Ages.* New York: Crossroad, 1992.

———. *Wisdom Distilled from the Daily: Living the Rule of St. Benedict Today.* San Francisco: Harper & Row, 1991.

Chodron, Pema. *The Places That Scare You: A Guide to Fearlessness in Difficult Times.* Boston: Shambhala Publications, 2001.

Clarke, John, OCD, trans. *Story of a Soul: The Autobiography of Saint Thérèse of Lisieux.* Washington, DC: ICS Publications, 1996.

Cleary, Thomas, trans. *Dhammapada: The Sayings of the Buddha.* New York: Bantam Books, 1994.

Colledge, Edmund, OSA, and James Walsh, SJ, trans. and introduction. *Julian of Norwich: Showings.* New York: Paulist Press, 1978.

Culligan, Kevin, OCD, and Regis Jordan, OCD, eds. *Carmel and Contemplation: Transforming Human Consciousness.* Carmelite Studies VIII. Washington, DC: ICS Publications, Institute of Carmelite Studies, 2000.

Culligan, Kevin, Mary Jo Meadow, and Daniel Chowning. *Purifying the Heart: Buddhist Insight Meditation for Christians.* New York: Crossroad, 1994.

Dalai Lama. *The Dalai Lama at Harvard.* Translated and edited by Jeffrey Hopkins. Ithaca, NY: Snow Lion Publications, 1988.

———. *A Flash of Lightning in the Dark of Night: A Guide to the Bodhisattva's Way of Life.* Boston: Shambhala Publications, 1994.

———. *Lojong: Training the Mind.* Boston: Wisdom Publications, 1999.

———. *Transforming the Mind: Teachings on Generating Compassion.* Edited by Dominique Side. Translated by Geshe Thupten Kinpa. London: Thorsons, 2000.

De Caussade, Jean Pierre. *Abandonment to Divine Providence.* Garden City, NY: Image Books / Doubleday, 1975.

——. *The Sacrament of the Present Moment.* Translated by Kitty Muggeridge. San Francisco: HarperCollins, 1989. First published 1966 as *L'Abandon à la Providence divine.*

De Chardin, Pierre Teilhard. *The Divine Milieu.* New York: Perennial Library/Harper & Row, 1960.

——. *The Phenomenon of Man.* New York: Perennial Library / Harper & Row, 1959. First published 1955 by Editions du Seuil, Paris.

De Mello, Anthony, SJ. *Awareness: The Perils and Opportunities of Reality; A De Mello Spirituality Conference in His Own Words.* New York: Image Books / Doubleday, 1992.

——. *Sadhana: A Way to God.* St. Louis, MO: The Institute of Jesuit Sources, 1978.

DeCharms, Christopher. *Two Views of Mind: Abhidharma and Brain Science.* Ithaca, NY: Snow Lion Publications, 1997.

Dodes, Lance. *The Heart of Addiction.* New York: HarperCollins, 2002.

Epstein, Mark. *Going to Pieces Without Falling Apart: A Buddhist Perspective on Wholeness; Lessons from Meditation and Psychotherapy.* New York: Broadway Books, 1998.

——. *Open to Desire: Embracing a Lust for Life: Insights from Buddhism and Psychotherapy.* New York: Gotham Books, 2005.

——. "The Psychodynamics of Meditation: Pitfalls on the Spiritual Path." *Journal of Transpersonal Psychology* 22, no. 1 (1990), 17–34.

——. *Thoughts Without a Thinker: Psychotherapy from a Buddhist Perspective.* New York: Basic Books / HarperCollins, 1995.

Feild, Reshad. *Steps to Freedom.* Putney, VT: Threshold Books, 1983.

Feldman, Christina. *Principles of Meditation.* London: Thorsons / HarperCollins, 1998.

Finley, James. *Merton's Palace of Nowhere: A Search for God through Awareness of the True Self.* Notre Dame, IN: Ave Maria Press, 1978.

Flickstein, Matthew. *Swallowing the River Ganges: A Practical Guide to the Path of Purification.* Boston: Wisdom Publications, 2001.

Fox, Matthew. *Breakthrough: Meister Eckhart's Creation Spirituality in New Translation.* Garden City, NY: Image Books, 1980.

———. *Meditations with Meister Eckhart.* Introduction and versions by Matthew Fox. Santa Fe, NM: Bear, 1982.

———. *Original Blessing: A Primer in Creation Spirituality.* Sante Fe, NM: Bear, 1983.

Franck, Frederick. *Zen Seeing, Zen Drawing: Meditation in Action.* New York: Bantam Books, 1993.

Freeman, Laurence. *Jesus the Teacher Within.* New York: Continuum, 2000.

Fritz, Robert. *The Path of Least Resistance: Learning to Become the Creative Force in Your Own Life.* New York: Ballantine Books, 1984.

———. *Your Life as Art.* Newfane, VT: Newfane Press, 2003.

Fronsdal, Gil. *The Issue at Hand: Essays on Buddhist Mindfulness Practice.* San Francisco: Insight Meditation Center of the Mid-Peninsula, 2001.

Funk, Robert W., Roy W. Hoover, and the Jesus Seminar. *The Five Gospels: What Did Jesus Really Say? The Search for the Authentic Words of Jesus.* San Francisco: HarperCollins, 1997.

Gendlin, Eugene T. *Focusing.* Rev. ed. New York: Bantam Books, 1981.

Goldstein, Joseph. *The Experience of Insight: A Simple and Direct Guide to Buddhist Meditation.* Boston: Shambhala Publications, 1983.

———. *Insight Meditation: The Practice of Freedom.* Boston: Shambhala Publications, 1994.

———. *One Dharma: The Emerging Western Buddhism.* San Francisco: Harper, 2002.

Goldstein, Joseph, and Jack Kornfield. *Seeking the Heart of Wisdom: The Path of Insight Meditation.* Boston: Shambhala Publications, 1987.

Goleman, Daniel. *Destructive Emotions: How Can We Overcome Them? A Scientific Dialogue with the Dalai Lama.* New York: Bantam Books, 2003.

Groeschel, Benedict J. *Spiritual Passages: The Psychology of Spiritual Development.* New York: Crossroad, 1984.

Gunaratana, Bhante Henepola. *Eight Mindful Steps to Happiness: Walking the Buddha's Path.* Boston: Wisdom Publications, 2001.

———. *Mindfulness in Plain English.* Boston: Wisdom Publications, 1992.

Gyatso, Geshe Kelsang. *Meaningful to Behold: The Bodhisattva's Way of Life.* London: Tharpa Publications, 1980.

Hafiz. *The Gift: Poems by Hafiz, The Great Sufi Master.* Translated by David Ladinsky. New York: Penguin, 1999.

Hanh, Thich Nhat. *Transformation and Healing: The Sutra on the Four Establishments of Mindfulness.* Berkeley, CA: Parallax Press, 1990.

Harrison, Gavin. *In the Lap of the Buddha.* Boston: Shambhala Publications, 1994.

Hays, Edward. *Pray All Ways.* Leavenworth, KS: Forest of Peace Publishing, 1981.

Henry, Patrick, ed. *Benedict's Dharma: Buddhists Reflect on the Rule of St. Benedict.* New York: Riverhead Books / Penguin Putnam, 2001.

Hick, John, and Paul F. Knitter, eds. *The Myth of Christian Uniqueness: Toward a Pluralistic Theology of Religions.* Maryknoll, NY: Orbis Books, 1987.

Hooks, Bell. *All About Love: New Visions.* New York: HarperCollins, 2000.

Hopkins, Jeffrey. *Meditation on Emptiness.* Boston: Wisdom Publications, 1983.

Hopkins, Jeffrey, et al., ed. and trans. *Compassion in Tibetan Buddhism.* Ithaca, NY: Snow Lion Publications, 1980.

Huxley, Aldous. *The Perennial Philosophy.* New York: Harper and Row, 1944.

Kabat-Zinn, Jon. *Full Catastrophe Living: Using the Wisdom of Your Body and Mind to Face Stress, Pain, and Illness.* New York: Delta, 1990.

Kabir. *The Kabir Book: Forty-Four of the Ecstatic Poems of Kabir.* Translated by Robert Bly. Boston: Beacon Press, 1971.

Katie, Byron. *Loving What Is: Four Questions That Can Change Your Life.* New York: Harmony Books, 2002.

Kavanaugh, Kieran, OCD, and Otilio Rodriguez, OCD, trans. *The Collected Works of St. John of the Cross.* Washington, DC: ICS Publications, Institute of Carmelite Studies, 1973.

Keating, Thomas. *Open Mind, Open Heart: The Contemplative Dimension of the Gospel.* New York: Continuum, 1994. Published 1986 by St. Benedict's Monastery.

Keenan, John P. *The Gospel of Mark: A Mahayana Reading.* Maryknoll, NY: Orbis Books, 1995.

Khema, Ayya. *When the Iron Eagle Flies: Buddhism for the West.* Boston: Wisdom Publications, 2000.

———. *Who Is My Self? A Guide to Buddhist Meditation.* Boston: Wisdom Publications, 1997.

Klein, Anne C. *Meeting the Great Bliss Queen: Buddhists, Feminists, and the Art of the Self.* Boston: Beacon Press, 1995.

———. *Path to the Middle.* Albany: State University of New York Press, 1994.

Kornfield, Jack. *Living Dharma: Teachings of Twelve Buddhist Masters.* Boston: Shambhala Publications, 1996. Originally published 1977 as *Living Buddhist Masters.*

———. *A Path with Heart: A Guide Through the Perils and Promises of Spiritual Life.* New York: Bantam Books, 1993.

———. *Teachings of the Buddha.* Rev. ed. Boston: Shambhala Publications, 1993.

Kramer, Greg. *Meditating Together, Speaking from Silence: The Practice of Insight Dialogue.* Portland, OR: Metta Foundation, 1999. (See also www.metta.org.)

Krishna, Gopi. *Kundalini: The Evolutionary Energy of Man.* Boston: Shambhala Publications, 1997.

Krishnamurti, J. *The First and Last Freedom.* Ojai, CA: Krishnamurti Foundation of America, 1954. Published 1975 by HarperCollins.

Lawrence, Brother. *The Practice of the Presence of God: With Spiritual Maxims.* Old Tappan, NJ: Revell, 1999. Reprint edition.

Levine, Peter. *Waking the Tiger: Healing Trauma: The Innate Capacity to Transform Overwhelming Experiences.* Berkeley, CA: North Atlantic Books, 1997.

Levine, Stephen. *A Gradual Awakening.* New York: Anchor Books, 1979.

———. *A Year to Live: How to Live This Year as If It Were Your Last.* New York: Bell Tower, 1997.

Levko, John J. *Cassian's Prayer for the 21st Century.* Scranton, PA: University of Scranton Press, 2000.

Macy, Joanna. *Mutual Causality in Buddhism and General Systems Theory: The Dharma of Natural Systems.* Albany: State University of New York Press, 1991.

———. *World as Lover, World as Self.* Berkeley, CA: Parallax Press, 1991.

Macy, Joanna, and Molly Young Brown. *Coming Back to Life: Practices to Reconnect Our Lives, Our World.* Gabriola Island, BC, Canada: New Society Publishers, 1998.

Mahasi Sayadaw. *The Progress of Insight: Through the Stages of Purification.* Translated by Nyanaponika Thera. Kandy, Sri Lanka: Buddhist Publication Society, 1985.

May, Gerald G. *Addiction and Grace: Love and Spirituality in the Healing of Addictions.* San Francisco: HarperCollins, 1988. First paperback edition 1991.

———. *The Awakened Heart: Living Beyond Addiction.* San Francisco: HarperCollins, 1991.

McBrien, Richard P. *Catholicism.* San Francisco: Harper & Row, 1981.

Meadow, Mary Jo. *Gentling the Heart: Buddhist Loving-Kindness Practice for Christians.* New York: Crossroad, 1994.

Merton, Thomas. *The Ascent to Truth.* New York: Harcourt Brace Jovanovich, 1981. First published 1951 by the Abbey of Our Lady of Gethsemani.

———. *New Seeds of Contemplation.* New York: New Directions, 1972. First published 1961 by the Abbey of Our Lady of Gethsemani, Inc.

————. *Thoughts in Solitude: Meditations on the Spiritual Life and Man's Solitude before God.* New York: Chapel Book / Dell, 1961. First published 1956 by the Abbey of Our Lady of Gethsemani.

Mood, John J.L. *Rilke on Love and Other Difficulties: Translations and Considerations of Rainer Maria Rilke.* New York: W. W. Norton, 1975.

Mott, Michael. *The Seven Mountains of Thomas Merton.* Boston: Houghton Mifflin, 1984.

Nagao, Gadjin. *The Foundational Standpoint of Madhyamika Philosophy.* Translated by John P. Keenan. Albany: State University of New York Press, 1989.

Nanamoli, Bhikkhu (original translation), and Bhikkhu Bodhi, trans. *The Middle Length Discourses of the Buddha: A New Translation of the* Majjhima Nikaya. Boston: Wisdom Publications, 1995.

Napper, Elizabeth. *Dependent Arising and Emptiness.* Boston: Wisdom Publications, 1989.

Nelson, John E. *Healing the Split: Integrating Spirit Into Our Understanding of the Mentally Ill.* Albany: State University of New York Press, 1994.

Nemeck, Francis Kelly, OMI, and Marie Theresa Coombs, Hermit. *O Blessed Night: Recovering from Addiction, Codependence, and Attachment based on the Insights of St. John of the Cross and Pierre Teilhard de Chardin.* New York: Alba House, Society of St. Paul, 1991.

Newland, Guy. *The Two Truths.* Ithaca, NY: Snow Lion Publications, 1992.

Nisargadatta Maharaj. *I Am That: Talks with Sri Nisargadatta.* Durham, NC: Acorn Press, 1988.

Nisker, Wes. *Buddha Nature: Evolution as a Practical Guide to Enlightenment.* New York: Bantam Books, 1998.

Norbu, Chogyal Namkhai. *Dzogchen: The Self-Perfected State.* Edited by Adriano Clemente. Translated by John Shane. Ithaca, NY: Snow Lion Publications, 1996.

Nouwen, Henri J. M. *The Way of the Heart.* New York: Ballantine Books, 1981.

————. *With Open Hands.* Notre Dame, IN: Ave Maria Press, 1972.

————. *The Wounded Healer.* Garden City, NY: Image Books / Doubleday, 1972.

Nyanaponika Thera. *Abhidhamma Studies: Researches in Buddhist Psychology.* Kandy, Sri Lanka: Buddhist Publication Society, 1949.

————. *The Heart of Buddhist Meditation.* York Beach, ME: Samuel Weiser, 1965.

Ouspensky, P. D. *The Psychology of Man's Possible Evolution.* New York: Random House, 1974.

Palmer, G. E. H., Philip Sherrard, and Kallistos Ware, ed. and trans. *The Philokalia: The Complete Text of St. Nikodimos of the Holy Mountain and St. Makarios of Corinth.* London: Faber and Faber, 1979.

Pandita, Sayadaw U. *In This Very Life: The Liberation Teachings of the Buddha.* Boston: Wisdom Publications, 1991.

Peck, M. Scott. *People of the Lie: The Hope for Healing Human Evil.* New York: Simon & Schuster, 1983.

Peers, E. Allison, trans. *Interior Castles — Saint Theresa of Avila.* Garden City, NY: Doubleday /Image Books, 1961.

Pennington, M. Basil, OCSO. *Centering Prayer: Renewing an Ancient Christian Prayer Form.* Garden City, NY: Doubleday / Image Books, 1980.

Piburn, Sidney, ed. *The Dalai Lama: A Policy of Kindness; An Anthology of Writings By and About the Dalai Lama.* Ithaca, NY: Snow Lion Publications, 1993.

Piyadassi Thera. *The Buddha's Ancient Path.* Kandy, Sri Lanka: Buddhist Publication Society, 1949.

Plattig, Michael, O. Carm. "Freedom to Souls: Spiritual Accompaniment According to the Carmelite Tradition," in *Tending the Holy: Spiritual Direction Across Traditions.* Edited by Norvene Vest. Harrisburg, PA: Morehouse Publishing, 2003.

Podvoll, Edward M. *Recovering Sanity: A Compassionate Approach to Understanding and Treating Psychosis.* Boston: Shambhala Publications, 2003.

Rabten, Geshe. *Echoes of Voidness.* London: Wisdom Publications, 1983.

Radier, Beatrice, ed. *The Cloud of Unknowing and Other Works.* London: Penguin Books, 1977.

Rahula, Walpola. *What the Buddha Taught.* New York: Grove Press, 1959.

Rees, Mary. *Going Beyond What You Believe to Be True — First Steps.* Online meditation course at www.citta101.org, 2004.

———. *Transforming the Power of Anger and Resentment: Self-Questioning Strategies.* Houston: Citta 101, 1994.

Rilke, Rainer Maria. *Rilke on Love and Other Difficulties: Translations and Considerations of Rainer Maria Rilke* by John J. L. Mood. New York: W.W. Norton, 1975.

Rinpoche, Kyabje Kalu. *Luminous Mind: The Way of the Buddha.* Boston: Wisdom Publications, 1997.

Roberts, Bernadette. *The Experience of No-Self: A Contemplative Journey.* Boston: Shambhala Publications, 1985.

Rohr, Richard. *Everything Belongs: The Gift of Contemplative Prayer.* New York: Crossroad, 1999.

Rosenberg, Larry. *Breath by Breath: The Liberating Practice of Insight Meditation.* Boston: Shambhala Publications, 1998.

Rumi. *Open Secret: Versions of Rumi.* Translated by John Moyne and Coleman Barks. Boston: Shambhala Publications, 1984.

Sacks, Oliver. *An Anthropologist on Mars: Seven Paradoxical Tales.* New York: Vintage Books, 1995.

———. *The Man Who Mistook His Wife for a Hat: And Other Clinical Tales.* New York: Touchstone Books, 1998.

Salzberg, Sharon. *Faith: Trusting Your Own Deepest Experience.* New York: Riverhead Books, 2002.

———. *Lovingkindness: The Revolutionary Art of Happiness.* Boston: Shambhala Publications, 1997.

Salzberg, Sharon, and Joseph Goldstein. *Insight Meditation: A Step-by-Step Guide on How to Meditate.* Boulder, CO: Sounds True, 2001.

Santorelli, Saki. *Heal Thyself: Lessons on Mindfulness in Medicine.* New York: Bell Tower, 1999.

Segal, Zindel V., J. Mark G. Williams, and John D. Teasdale. *Mindfulness-Based Cognitive Therapy for Depression: A New Approach to Preventing Relapse.* New York: Guilford Press, 2002.

Shah, Idries. *Learning How to Learn: Psychology and Spirituality in the Sufi Way.* New York: Penguin, 1996.

Shantideva, Acharya. *Bodhisattvacharyavatara — A Guide to the Bodhisattva's Way of Life.* Translated by Stephen Batchelor. Dharmsala: Library of Tibetan Works and Archives, 1979.

Silananda, U. *The Four Foundations of Mindfulness.* Boston: Wisdom Publications, 1990.

Smith, Rodney. *Lessons from the Dying.* Boston: Wisdom Publications, 1998.

Soma Thera. *The Way of Mindfulness: Satipatthana Sutta Commentary.* Kandy, Sri Lanka: Buddhist Publication Society, 1941.

Sumedho, Ajahn. *The Way It Is.* Amaravati Buddhist Monastery, Great Gaddesden, UK: Amaravati Publications, 1991.

Suzuki, Shunryu. *Zen Mind, Beginner's Mind.* New York: Weatherhill, 1970.

Swidler, Leonard, ed. *Toward a Universal Theology of Religion.* Maryknoll, NY: Orbis Books, 1988.

Talbot, Michael. *The Holographic Universe.* New York: HarperCollins, 1991.

Teilhard de Chardin, Pierre. *The Divine Milieu.* New York: Harper & Row, 1960. First published 1957 as *Le Milieu Divin.*

———. *The Phenomenon of Man.* New York: Harper & Row, 1959. Originally published 1955 as *Le Phénomene Humain.*

Thompson, Helen, BVM. *Journey Toward Wholeness: A Jungian Model of Adult Spiritual Growth.* New York: Paulist Press, 1982.

Titmuss, Christopher. *Light on Enlightenment: Revolutionary Teachings on the Inner Life.* Boston: Shambhala Publications, 1999.

Tolle, Eckhart. *The Power of Now: A Guide to Spiritual Enlightenment.* Novato, CA: New World Library, 1999.

Toner, Jules J. *A Commentary on St. Ignatius' Rules for the Discernment of Spirits.* St. Louis, MO: The Institute of Jesuit Sources, 1982.

Trungpa, Chogyam. *Cutting Through Spiritual Materialism*. Boston: Shambhala Publications, 1973.

Tweedie, Irina. *The Chasm of Fire: A Woman's Experience with the Teachings of a Sufi Master*. Reissue ed. Shaftsbury, Dorset, UK: Element Books, 1993.

Vanier, Jean. *From Brokenness to Community*. Mahwah, NJ: Paulist Press, 1992.

Von Bruck, Michael. "Buddhist Sunyata and the Christian Trinity: The Emerging Holistic Paradigm" in *Buddhist Emptiness and Christian Trinity: Essays and Exploration*. Edited by Roger Corless and Paul F. Knitter. New York: Paulist Press, 1990.

Walsh, John. *Evangelization and Justice: New Insights for Christian Ministry*. Maryknoll, NY: Orbis Books, 1982.

Walsh, Roger. *Staying Alive: The Psychology of Human Survival*. Boulder, CO: New Science Library, Shambhala Publications, 1984.

Walsh, Roger, and Frances Vaughan. "The Art of Transcendence: An Introduction to Common Elements of Transpersonal Practices." *Journal of Transpersonal Psychology* 25, no. 1 (1993).

Walshe, Maurice, trans. *The Long Discourses of the Buddha: A Translation of the* Digha Nikaya. Boston: Wisdom Publications, 1995. First published 1987 as *Thus Have I Heard: The Long Discourses of the Buddha*.

Wangyal, Tenzin. *Healing with Form, Energy and Light: The Five Elements in Tibetan Shamanism, Tantra, and Dzogchen*. Ithaca, NY: Snow Lion Publications, 2002.

Ward, Benedicta, SLG, trans. *The Sayings of the Desert Fathers*. Kalamazoo, MI: Cistercian Publications, 1975.

Watts, Alan. *The Wisdom of Insecurity*. New York: Pantheon Books, 1951.

Weisman, Arinna, and Jean Smith. *The Beginner's Guide to Insight Meditation*. New York: Bell Tower, 2001.

Welwood, John, ed. *Awakening the Heart: East/West Approaches to Psychotherapy and the Healing Relationship*. Boston: New Science Library, Shambhala Publications, 1983.

———. *Journey of the Heart: The Path of Conscious Love.* New York: Harper Perennial, 1990.

———. *Toward a Psychology of Awakening: Buddhism, Psychotherapy, and the Path of Personal and Spiritual Transformation.* Boston: Shambhala Publications, 2000.

Wilber, Ken, Jack Engler, and Daniel P. Brown. *Transformations of Consciousness: Conventional and Contemplative Perspectives on Development.* Boston: Shambhala Publications, 1986.

Williams, Angel Kyodo. *Being Black: Zen and the Art of Living with Fearlessness and Grace.* New York: Viking Compass, 2000.

Zajonc, Arthur, ed. *The New Physics and Cosmology: Dialogues with the Dalai Lama.* New York: Oxford University Press, 2004.

About the Author

Mary Rees, MS, has been teaching since 1970. She worked for twenty years in public education as a teacher, a consultant, and an educational diagnostician, over time making a natural progression from teaching learning strategies to working with skillful qualities of mind and states of consciousness (which include ethical behavior and prayer).

The purpose of her work is to walk with others toward wholeness. She is involved primarily with people who want to be happy and at ease in life. Those who come to her classes often feel a little out of place in traditional settings (religious or secular). Many are dismayed at the moral and ethical state of the current culture and its institutions. They often remain faithful to their birth traditions or return to them with renewed enthusiasm. Mary also works with those in leadership roles within various traditions.

Mary is trained as a Spiritual Director, having completed a three-year program at the Cenacle Retreat House and the University of St. Thomas in Houston, Texas in 1990. She is also a community Dharma Leader in the Insight Meditation network and has been teaching Insight Meditation since 1989. Besides holding a master's degree in Specific Learning Disabilities, she has graduate hours in Christian Spirituality and Buddhist Meditation Theory.

You can learn more about Mary's work from her websites at www.citta101.org and www.maryrees.com.

I have repeatedly been asked how it is that I can be a Christian Spiritual Director, a Buddhist practitioner, and a meditation teacher. I understand the question and appreciate the concern as well as the confusion behind it. I struggled with the question a long time in my own spiritual work and have had many wonderful guides along the way. Now I can happily say there is no conflict—and I can explain why and, more importantly, describe how to begin. In this book, I invite the readers to explore Buddhist practice and see for themselves that it is actually a very powerful way of becoming Christian and also a way simply for anyone to be free, happy, and at ease in life, no matter what the circumstances or belief.

— MARY REES

Nutshell

PUBLICATIONS

Large topics in brief
Small topics in depth

Educational materials
(especially for development of consciousness
for personal and spiritual unfoldment)

NUTSHELL PUBLICATIONS™
HOUSTON, TX
www.nutpub.com